# HOW TO READ TAROT

HEEL of FORTUNE.

THE FOOL.

THE HERMIT.

THE EMPE

# HOW TO READ
# TAROT
## —A MODERN GUIDE—

Jessica Wiggan

ALTHEA
PRESS

Interior and Cover Designer: Joshua Moore
Art Producer: Mike Hardgrove
Editor: Pam Kingsley
Production Editor: Andrew Yackira

ISBN: Print 978-1-64152-439-1 | eBook 978-1-64152-440-7

R2

This book is dedicated to my ancestors and guides who have paved the way for me to be able to share my voice, knowledge, and passion here and in other ways. Also to those who are stepping out of their comfort zones to fearlessly pursue their passions and share their gifts and light with the world. Your vulnerability is your strength—keep going.

# CONTENTS

# INTRODUCTION

**H**i to everyone! I can't even begin to express how excited I am to share my passion and study of the tarot with you. This feels like it has been building in my life for some time, but without my knowing that it would come to a moment like this—where I'd be able to provide a resource for others to use and grow from. I know I would have loved and benefited from a book like this at the start of my own tarot card–shuffling journey!

For me, tarot has always been intimate and personal, and I was lucky to start young under the loving guidance of my mother. When I was around age 13, she took me to have my cards read by an amazing elder who lived in Florida. I watched the woman as she shuffled and pulled cards for me, seeming to actually feel what I was feeling simply by looking at what unfolded. Well, after that experience I was hooked. I asked for my first tarot deck and was gifted one soon after. Twenty years later, I haven't stopped shuffling and growing.

It's my belief that there are gifts within each of us from a higher source—the Divine, as I like to call it. Also hidden in our heart and subconscious is a locked box that holds our destiny and fate, our truest desires, potential, and areas of weakness that—if we're comfortable exploring them—will turn into strengths. The tarot is one of many powerful tools you have at your disposal to unlock that box and discover what is protected within. When you connect with a source larger than just your physical and mental self, you connect with unlimited potential. The tarot is a way of communicating with that higher source outside of your prayers, meditation, and intentions.

Like anything involving symbols, intuition, and spirituality, in tarot, there is an abundance of space for you to work with your own interpretations. By looking at the images found in the cards, certain things will stand out to you on different days or with different questions. That was intended by the original creators of the tarot and also by our ascended masters—the people who lived before us and, through their experiences, helped pave the way for the rest of us through their deep spiritual experiences. They taught us to look for meaning in our everyday environment.

The knowledge of these symbols has stayed pretty consistent through the years and crosses the boundaries of many different traditions and cultures. This knowledge has been protected and passed down to each generation. Now you have the chance to hold these ancient symbols in your hands and see the same things the ancients saw, feel the same inspirations they felt, and hear the same messages they heard. You can choose to see those messages for yourself and develop your gifts privately, or you can share it with others if you are comfortable and ready. This is the beauty of the tarot.

For this reason (and many others), it is an honor to be able to share a piece of my life's study of the tarot in this book designed for people who are just as hungry to learn and explore the cards as I was and still am. I still see myself growing and discovering as I shuffle. That's the gift I hope you give yourself—to take the time, effort, and energy to explore your own gifts and to give the cards a chance to speak to you when you need them.

I encourage you to take your time with this book and your cards. Browse these pages at your leisure. Don't feel pressure to remember everything all at once. Keep the book close each time you pull your cards out; it will act as a guide to support you along your tarot journey. What makes this book different is that it provides you with the resources to understand the tarot's language as well as the space to add to what the cards will uniquely communicate to you, exclusively. This is on purpose, for your spiritual journey is yours alone; no one other than you can make it or shape it into anything. My intention is for this book to empower you to do just that!

My last note is this: I want you to know that there is a whole tribe of people—like you and me—who grow with the tarot every day and are excited to pour themselves into the cards. I say this because, with this book, you are welcomed into this circle of like-minded souls and spirits, and you'll never be alone in your study. My mother, the shaman and High Priestess, always said, "When the student is ready, the master will appear," as well as "If you build it, they will come," and that is what is happening for you. There is a reason for everything, and when you decided to dive into your study of the tarot, you sent a signal out to the universe that you were ready to transform, and instantly you were welcomed into our "love and light" soul family! With that, know that you are not alone on your journey! Reach out through Spirit or connect when you are ready. In the meantime, I wish you good luck and all the blessings in your studies, and I'm sure we'll cross paths along our journey!

Let's get started!

# PART I

# TAROT READING 101

# 1
# GETTING STARTED

**E**VERY JOURNEY BEGINS WITH A SINGLE STEP, so that's where we will begin now—with the very first step! As intimidating as the entire journey may seem (there are 78 cards in the deck, 156 total if you factor in reversed card meanings), you'll be surprised how fast you will learn not only about the cards but also about yourself when you break it down bit by bit.

I don't expect you to memorize the meanings of each card in full detail, but I do want you to become comfortable enough with them so that you can use your intuition along with this book as a guide or resource to give the best readings to yourself, your friends, and even your clients. With this book, you'll see how the tarot is equal parts complex and simple. Our study together will allow you to dive deep into the cards while still feeling supported and giving you the space to stretch and build your own intuitive muscle!

## HOW TO USE THE TAROT

The first thing to discuss is the importance of your relationship with the tarot. What makes the tarot so different from another random deck of cards, and why would you even want to consider placing your future or decision-making into the tarot's hands? The tarot is far more than just a card deck used for entertainment; it is a powerful tool for divination, self-discovery, and magick. If used properly, the cards can deepen your spiritual connection and knowledge of self, help you develop your intuitive capabilities, and help you become more aware of your external and internal environments.

Tarot can be used for both good and evil. You should use the cards only for good always—that is, to empower yourself or others with knowledge to move forward for your highest and greatest good. Using the tarot for bad or evil intent includes:

- Prying into the details of someone's private life.
- Abusing the cards by continually shuffling and ignoring their messages and your own intuitive wisdom.
- Using them to send ill intent to others.

You never want to harm anyone— including yourself. Only you can assess if you are abusing the deck or energy, and it will be up to you to re-center and regain balance.

My personal goal is help you become so connected to your own intuitive knowledge and third eye wisdom (your intuition and inner knowing ingrained within you) that the use of the tarot will merely become a booster tool to strengthen and support the answers you already know.

## TAROT AND YOU

Your relationship with the tarot can easily become one of the most meaningful and trusted in your life. It has the potential to be a trusted confidant; it has no ulterior motives. Its purpose is to give you clear and precise advice and insight, and it can see things that you—and others—can't. Of course the tarot can't replace your relationships with others, but if used correctly, it can absolutely help you relate to and understand people and your environment better, and it can help you accomplish your goals, no matter what they are.

In my own journey, I gravitated toward a tarot deck designed around goddess energy because, at the time, I was working on self-love and stepping into my own personal power. This deck would quickly become one of my closest "friends," helping guide me through an emotional and transformative time. I shuffled multiple times a day every day, asking everything from the simplest to the most complex questions. I wrote down all of those questions in my tarot journal and would frequently return to those questions days or weeks (and then finally years) later to review what I had pulled for myself and compare that to what actually occurred. (I'll talk about keeping a tarot journal later.)

The insight of the cards was continuously astounding, and I quickly learned that not only do they show you the energy of the question at the moment, but they also provide a look into the future, offer insight and advice, and definitely sprinkle in some humor. You'll see your own deck has a "voice" and attitude all its own, and sometimes a good reading is the rude shove you needed to get moving . . . the cards will definitely provide that!

The cards' messages for me were always quiet but powerful, and I would have been wise to listen to them the first time, no matter what they were trying to tell me. The outcome the tarot hinted toward always unfolded as originally predicted. I'm known to be stubborn, but it didn't take me long to realize that I could use the cards to discover the obstacles in my path as well as the opportunities here or soon to come and work to change my steps so they matched what I wanted for myself—if I could control it. For the things I couldn't control or change, it gave me confirmation to "let go and let God," meaning to release my grip on the situation and open up to being completely guided each step of the way.

The cards were the first ones to let me know what was on the horizon and how to prepare for it—I just needed to listen. This helped build my faith in the universe and in myself. It's my goal now to help you be in a space where you can help yourself through the tarot and maybe, if you choose, to work with tarot to help others.

## Getting to Know Your Cards

If you are going to trust the cards enough to provide guidance and insight into your life, then it's super important that you take time to get to know them and for them to get to understand you. As with any relationship, there needs to be trust of some kind before you share your secrets. You can ask intimate questions of a new deck, but you want to make sure you understand the language your cards will be speaking. Their guidance and insight will be useless if you don't understand what they're saying.

It doesn't matter if you are a beginner or an advanced tarot reader; there is *always* something to discover in the cards. The cards are filled with symbolism, and different aspects will jump out during different readings. This is part of their magick. You'll discover how one card's repeated appearance in your life has a special meaning that deviates from what you have traditionally learned about that card. Be open to these revelations because it's important to your growth and journey with your cards. You'll find yourself having many aha moments and revelations—delivered in a straight-ahead manner, just like the Judgement card delivers its message!

To start getting to know your cards, I suggest breaking the deck into two parts, the Major and Minor Arcana (see part two for specifics on each of these cards). Flip through each card within each section, and in a notebook that you designate as your tarot journal, make a note of the symbolism, feelings, and thoughts that are triggered as you examine each card. For example, looking at The Tower card, what memories or events in life does it remind you of? As you work with the tarot, revisit your initial notes of what stood out to you and how they apply to you in that moment. You'll start to notice trends and also specific messages that the angels and your spirit guides are trying to reveal to you.

Just like any important relationship, what you put into the tarot is what you will get out of it. If developing and growing your tarot skills are important to you, practice often, if not daily. If you neglect your cards, you will find your growth with them—and even your feeling of being guided in life—stunted.

Lastly, step outside your comfort zone when it comes to the questions you ask the cards. The cards will answer whatever you ask in the best way they know how, so you want to "try on" different ways of asking the tarot for its insight and guidance. For example, if you normally ask what or when something is going to happen, switch your question to "How can I make this happen?" or "What advice can you give me to reach my desired outcome?" and let them speak to you in the way only they can. This will help connect you to your cards even further because you will learn to trust in the cards' insight and messages as well as how to communicate with them to make the best decisions possible.

## HOW DOES THE TAROT WORK?

Tarot is a medium to connect with whatever source you choose, but most use it to connect with their spirit guides, angels, or inner wisdom for clarity and guidance in regard to a specific question. Some even use it to spy on others. But remember the laws of karma: What you do to others will come back to you, so try not to use these cards for doing dirty work or anything else that could be considered less than positive, no matter how tempting it is!

*Continued on page 9*

# Reading for Yourself

The best way to get familiar with the cards is the simplest: Pull one or two cards for yourself daily and keep a journal of all your readings! This is what I have done for years, and it has served me well. It's something I always recommend to the students in my tarot school when they are diving into their own decks.

Your own personal questions and card pulls are perfect ways to get used to working with the tarot, learning how to listen to and communicate with them, and strengthening your intuitive muscle.

Doing daily tarot draw pulls and keeping a journal to record each card pulled, the basic meaning of the card, and what that message means for you in that moment will help you get familiar with the cards really fast. The saying "hindsight is always 20/20" applies to these types of practices; by reviewing the past entries, you'll see how the cards showed you glimpses of what was approaching.

When you are working with daily draws, keep your mind open and try to refrain from always asking the cards a question (or the same question multiple times). Give them the space to tell you what you need to be aware of for that day. You'll see that the cards pick up on an undercurrent of energy that will sometimes reveal an event to you weeks before it occurs, despite your focusing on something else for your card pull. This is another reason why you'll want to practice working with the tarot; you'll start to intuitively sense timing or messages, and this is not something you can rush or force.

# Tarot's Relationship with Numerology, Astrology, and the Kabbalah

I want to make it clear that everything is symbolic within the tarot and no detail should be overlooked or dismissed. This is why later in the book I go into the symbolism of each of the cards; it all connects. The predominant symbolism is numerology and astrology, but in traditional decks like the Rider-Waite, you will see the appearance of Kabbalah, the ancient Jewish tradition of mystical interpretation that helps us discover purpose and meaning in our lives.

Numerology is the use of numbers to divine meaning in something, including the tarot. For example, examine The Emperor from the Major Arcana—he is the face of the number 4. In numerology, 4 is considered to be masculine energy, as is The Emperor. The number 4 gives both strength and stability but this number is also *very* stubborn and doesn't budge. Does this sound like an emperor at all? When you see him show up in a reading, the energy and elements of *all* those symbols come out to play. They are chosen by your guides for a reason.

Now, look at the other "number 4" cards within the deck and notice how they are *all* similar, although totally different because they are ruled by different elements: water (emotion), air (mind, intellect), earth (grounding, security), and fire (energy).

Let's walk through it:

**Four of Cups:** Bored. Discontent. Not budging emotionally. Sitting still. Unamused.

**Four of Swords:** Stillness. Rest. Needing time. Not moving.

**Four of Pentacles:** Grounded. Not budging. Selfish. Hoarding.

**Four of Wands:** Rejoicing within the current moment. Happy with status quo. Celebrating the now, but also not apt to move yet.

They are each ruled by the energy of their number *and* their element.

When doing a reading, look for common themes within the spread. Are there many repeating numbers or energies? That tells a lot about the situation, just as looking into an astrology chart does. It is all connected.

Continued from page 6

Because the tarot has potential for misuse, throughout history, people have feared it or linked it to negativity when in reality it is the user's intention that affects how it will work. For example, if you have a hammer and use that hammer to build homes for people, then your intent is good. But if you use the same hammer to break a car window to steal a wallet on the front seat, your intent is bad. It is your intention—not the tool—that creates the outcome of good or evil.

By calling in Spirit, you give permission to these forces to share their knowledge with you in a way that you can see and feel through your intuition, which is something we all have. Your guides will work to choose the cards that best reflect the energy surrounding your question to help provide you with better understanding. From there, you are empowered to make a decision that helps move you toward your desired outcome.

If your guides see that there is something in your environment you need to be made aware of, they will notify you of it, which you'll witness in "jumping cards," cards that seem to mysteriously jump from the deck or continue to appear in pulls in an attempt to make themselves known to you. This is where the divinatory side of the tarot occurs, by revealing parts of the future so you can reroute or move accordingly, if that's what you want to do. The cards are literally in your hands.

## What Can a Reading Reveal?

As much as the tarot can and will reveal, there are certain things it simply will not touch on. This is for your own highest and greatest good. As humans, there are lessons and things we need to experience in this life that are unavoidable for our best interests. It may not make sense at the time or it may seem negative in the moment, but their purpose is designed to teach us the most powerful lessons possible in the time we have here on earth. You'll find that some questions you ask may have cloudy answers or may not make sense. This is because a clear answer is not in your best interest at the time and you must experience the lesson for what it is, trust your judgment, and stay open to life's process.

The tarot will also not allow you to pry into areas that are considered off-limits: like questions that are too invasive into another person's life, areas you need to navigate into and figure out for yourself, or questions you stubbornly keep asking again and again. Even the cards can get exhausted with repeated questions, so choose a time and create a sacred space. Focus when you pull, and then journal what you see and what the cards tell you. Give the outcome some time and space to unfold, and revisit your notes later to see how things have revealed themselves.

Also, not everything is a clear and definitive yes or no answer. The tarot is notorious for being cryptic with its answers to some questions, especially when it comes to matters like timing. This is because many factors can come into play and change the course for you or others. Tarot understands that not all things are black or white—there needs to be some room for gray and unclear answers. Respect what the tarot is suggesting and try not to force an answer from the cards. You'll see their frustration when you don't accept the original answer they've given or when you ask about something they don't want you to hear or know now. This is for your own protection, especially if you set the intention that the cards share messages for your highest and greatest good. (I'll discuss more about that later.)

## Can the Cards Predict the Future?

The tarot can absolutely reveal the future. But it's important to understand the future is something you can create and change, especially if the cards show that your current path is leading in a direction you don't want to go. Because the tarot reveals the energy of everything that is around the question you have asked (depending on the spread you are using), you can plainly see where you are headed if things continue as they are. The beauty of this is that, again, if you are not happy with where you are headed, you can change it . . . and you can even ask the cards to give you advice about what you can start to do now to change your course.

Some circumstances can't be changed, and usually that is for your highest and greatest good. For example, say you are stuck in a relationship that isn't good for you. You are still motivated to make it work, but your partner doesn't share the same ambition. The cards will show you the truth of that and may suggest that a split is inevitable or offer some other solution. Because they have shown you the future, you can choose to continue to fight for the relationship or walk away, but no matter what your action, the outcome remains the same.

My favorite approach is to ask my question and pull the cards out in a spread; my go-to is the Celtic Cross (see page 172). I'll see all aspects of what is around me and the question. Then I will follow up and ask the cards for advice regarding what I can do now to help things progress in a way I feel will be successful for me or to reroute if I don't like where the cards tell me I am headed. I'm also known to ask my guides to speak out and tell me if there are other things I need to hear or look out for. I have learned over time that sometimes what I want for myself in this moment may be less than what I deserve . . . or that the universe has something far better in store for me.

Giving the cards the chance to reveal hidden blessings has placed me in positions to be open to miracles and opportunities that I would never have thought to ask for. Let the same be true for you—ask about your future but be flexible about what you expect and about the advice the cards give you.

## What is My Role as a Reader?

Your role as a reader is to translate the message of the cards without passing judgment or making suggestions as to what the querent (the person who is asking the question) should do, unless they clearly ask.

Still, it's important for both you and the querent to remember that whatever they choose to do is ultimately their decision and they should always follow their intuition. This sounds easy enough, but you'll find it can be difficult, especially in the moments when the cards reveal challenging messages or the querent is hell-bent on doing things their way, despite what the cards have revealed to them. It is what it is. At the end of the day, remember that this is their life to live and that because they are human and here to have an experience, they will face situations that will test them for the good of their own growth. What may seem obvious to you is not necessarily what they are destined for, and it is up to them to decide what actions to take.

Your role as a reader is also to separate yourself—your hopes, expectations, and wishes for the querent and the reading—from the reading and from the message that is delivered to the querent. When you are working with the cards, let them speak through you, no matter how pure your intention is. Again, this is easier said than done, especially when you care for the people you are reading for.

When you are giving the reading, it is your responsibility to step firmly into the role as a reader so that messages are never mixed, and the querent receives pure advice from Spirit to help guide them along their way. Again, Spirit and the tarot can see the things that we as readers sometimes can't, so rely only on your intuition and cards to share messages during the reading. If you can't do this, consider reading solely for yourself for the time being until you are ready to read for others.

# 2

# HOW TO GIVE
# READINGS

**N**OW LET'S DISCUSS WHAT READING FOR others and yourself should and will look like. First things first, you are going to need to incorporate self-protection. This can look different for each reader, but I'll share with you my process. Then I'll cover helping you or your client with phrasing questions in a way that the cards can best serve you its answers. (This seems simple enough, but you'd be surprised how this part can tie knots that complicate the entire reading!) And I'll address other issues you may have or could encounter. Pulling cards for others is very exciting, and with these tools, you'll be able to give others the best reading and insight possible! Let's get started!

## READING FOR OTHERS

It almost seems inevitable that at some point someone is going to ask you to read for them after they find out that you have an interest in working with the tarot. In my own journey, the first thing I wanted to do was to selfishly shuffle and ask a few questions for myself and then soon after I wanted to shuffle and pull for everyone and anyone around me.

This is all exciting and natural, but it's important to learn what that process should look like to protect you as well as the people you are reading for. Even when your intentions and the intentions of others are pure, it is important to protect yourself and others while simultaneously giving a good reading. Most people take the advice of tarot very seriously, so when sharing tarot messages with others, it's important to do it responsibly. At the same time, the person you are reading for will bring their own unique energies to the reading, which can affect you in positive and negative ways. It's not uncommon to give a reading to someone and feel what they are feeling when it comes to their question. If you are not grounded and protected before you start the reading, you can find yourself taking on that emotional burden. They walk away feeling refreshed, leaving you drained, weeping, and exhausted!

This was one of my own biggest trials with sharing my gifts with others. My heart wanted to help people in their moments of anxiety and fear—and I did—but afterward, it felt like I had absorbed their energy into my own during our session. Let's prevent this from happening to you by discussing how you can protect yourself while giving amazing readings to others as well as to yourself.

## GROUNDING, PROTECTION, AND CLEANSING

The simplest, most basic forms of reading preparation for yourself as well as for others is grounding, protection, and cleansing. Grounding is the process where you calm and center yourself so that nothing disturbs or disrupts your peace and balance from within. This is important for two main reasons. First, readings are often emotionally charged. Grounding and centering prepare you for such moments so you can maintain your focus and clarity while clearly delivering the message of the cards.

Also, most people working with the tarot have set the intention to invite Spirit or angelic guides to communicate with them through the cards. Because you are working with the spirit realms, it's important to take the time to ground yourself or you can find yourself feeling dazed, losing focus, or even having a sensation of floating on a cloud or being out of touch with reality or the rest of the world. As wonderful as it may sound to float on a cloud, it is best for you to keep a healthy boundary between you and the spirit world so that you are able to live effectively and serve your purpose to others here on earth.

Protection is also incredibly important. This is where you call in your spirit guides to protect you while you work with the spirit realms. When it comes to whom or what you should call in for protection, it varies depending on your personal belief system, but I have always asked for Divine Source and the protection of the angels to work with me and guide me. I have never in all my years as a professional tarot reader had any evil or bad things happen during or because of a reading; this is because I never miss the chance to call in protection for myself and my clients. In fact, all my readings have been constructive and empowering, even when the cards have revealed difficult messages or outcomes that didn't match the querent's desires or wishes. The same will be true for you if you take the time to call in for protection.

After the reading is completed and the messages from the tarot have been received, it is important to cleanse your deck. It doesn't matter if you have been reading for yourself or for others; over time energy, vibes, emotion, and lingering questions will build up on your cards and influence the outcome of future readings. For this reason, you should cleanse your deck, as discussed next, often,

to ensure that nothing prevents the cards from giving accurate readings.

## Purifying Smoke and Crystals

One of my favorite ways to cleanse my deck is to use the smoke from sage, palo santo, or incense. Using purifying smoke during my cleansing ritual is not only quick and easy, it's highly powerful and effective in removing lingering vibes or energies that, over time, can stick to the deck or even to you. After every reading, I will use something light like the smoke from incense or palo santo and say a simple prayer to "hit the reset button" on the card deck.

Let's break down the different types of smoke and why you would want to use each of them:

**Incense** tends to be the lightest smoke and it's what I use to cleanse and purify the deck after each reading. I personally gravitate toward scents like lavender or sandalwood although I have many friends in the tarot community that find themselves gravitating toward heavier scents like frankincense and myrrh, sage, or patchouli.

**Palo santo** is another excellent way to cleanse the deck after readings. Palo santo allows positive vibes and blessings to continue to linger, versus sage, which functions as a total detox, wiping the deck clean. Palo santo is a good choice if you are using one deck solely for readings for yourself as it is only your energy that you bring to the cards, and there's no need to "power cleanse" it. You can use palo santo on a more regular basis, occasionally opting for a deeper cleanse with sage.

**Sage** is one of the spiritual power cleansers, best used for a "total reset," as it wipes the deck clean of all energies. You'll know this is needed when the energy of the cards just feels "off": maybe you keep pulling the same cards, or maybe you've had a really intense emotional reading and you need a deep clean to make sure the messages of that reading don't spill over into your next one. Because I work with the tarot so often, I use sage at least once every two weeks, or around every twenty readings or so, but you can sage as often as you choose. If I have a particularly emotional or spiritually heavy reading, I will sage myself, my space, and the deck right afterward. Sage will totally remove lingering energy—good or bad—and give a blank slate for you to start fresh in.

The second-best way to cleanse the cards is to use crystals, although there are many who prefer crystals to purifying smoke. Quartz crystal, for example, is amazing at cleansing the deck's energy, and is one of my favorites. Once a month I will place a crystal over my deck under the light of the full moon with the intention of charging the deck up with lunar energy or purifying it. This keeps the vibes of me, my deck, and my space high and clear. I have never given a bad or confused reading and I attribute this to cleansing my deck regularly under a new or full moon with crystals.

Keeping crystals around you while you work can also help guard the energy of the room you are reading in. Amethyst, quartz, rose quartz, and spirit quartz are the crystals spiritual workers find themselves working with the most: not only are they easy to find and affordable, they are also powerful for protection and for helping channel messages through angels and Spirit. Working with crystals nearby is an effortless way to change the vibration of the room you are working in and to help you connect fully with your guides.

## Ask for Protection

You don't always need objects to protect you during readings. In fact, I feel the best way to protect yourself—whether or not you use sage, crystals, incense, etc.—is by calling in Divine Source energy or your angels to guard you while you work. Words are powerful, as is intention, and when you ask for healing and guidance, it will always instantly be delivered to you. In fact, any-thing you could ever need can be summoned simply by asking for it through prayer or intention.

One of my favorite prayers is to ask for spirit guides from the highest lights of the universe to work with me and through me to deliver messages for my highest and greatest good. Doing this ensures you are never making yourself available to lower energies that may try to move the reading into a negative space or confuse or misguide you. When you are working with your personal spirit guides, they will pick and choose the best methods to help you along your path and are quick to find the most comfortable way to communicate. If that is the tarot, they are happy to oblige. You'd be stunned how much they are willing to share to open your eyes to blessings and opportunities all around you.

You can call in protection from your guides out loud, quietly, or in your head—just make sure that you are clearly asking for the highest protection possible and for guidance that is in your best interest as well as anyone you are reading for.

## READING 101

Okay, we've covered the bones and foundation of a reading—now it's time to break into how to actually do it. The process begins with shuffling, cutting the deck, and pulling the cards. I'll guide you through this process, and then we'll explore reversed cards, and I'll help you decide whether or not you'd like to work with them. Every reader is different, so everyone's methods will be different, but there are a few things that tend to remain consistent for all of us.

### Shuffling

As simple as it may seem, the question I get asked most often is about how to shuffle the cards. Is there a special way to shuffle them? For me, it depends on the size of the card deck and also what my intention is. You always want to shuffle in a way that feels the most comfortable and best for you.

At the simplest level, some cards are larger than the average card deck, so shuffling can be difficult. In such cases, I sort through each one facedown on the table and place them in three separate piles, focusing on my question. Separating the cards into three piles is also a way to bless the deck further; I don't start a reading without this additional level of blessing.

For my average-size card decks, I shuffle them in my hands in whatever way feels best. There are many readers who shuffle as they would a typical deck of cards; there are those who only shuffle by spreading them out and hand selecting each card for their reading; and there are those who shuffle them in their hands. All of these methods are perfect as long as you are comfortable and you are giving the cards a chance to sort and mix themselves.

The only thing you need to focus on during the shuffling process is the question you are asking. Keep shuffling and concentrating on your question until you intuitively feel that the answer is ready within the cards. Cut the deck into three piles to bless it, place the cards back together in the way that feels best for you, and then pull your cards out to set up the spread to start the reading. If you are reading for someone else and don't know the question, focus on their energy and ask your spirit guides for their blessing and protection to provide the messages the querent needs to hear at the moment in time.

## Navigating Querent Questions

When reading for others, I give my querent the opportunity to share their question with me, but I never demand it or require it. Usually, you are dealing with very sensitive areas of someone's life, so there are many who choose to go to a reader but also have a need to guard or protect their question. This is fine. You are there to serve as a messenger, and you have to remember that the goal of the reading is to provide a message to help the querent in the way that best serves them. If they need to ask their question and keep it private, let it be so.

Oftentimes, you will get a sense of what their question could be in reference to by looking at the energy of the cards that are placed within the spread. For example, if you see a lot of Pentacles cards, you can pretty much tell that that person is asking about investments, career, security, or work, while many Cups cards can show how concerned someone is about matters of the heart, feelings, healing, or love. Deliver the message as best as you can while remaining respectful of their space and distance.

In my experience, a lot of people start the reading on guard, but as we move along—usually after I've shared pieces of what I see for them—they "confess" what they asked and what they are thinking and feeling. They can sense that I've created a sacred, safe space for them to pour their heart out to me, and when they are ready and the reading resonates, they bloom like a flower right in front of my eyes!

What helps this to occur is the fact that I let them do what is comfortable for them. I'm patient and honest, and, because of this, they feel safe. They also know that I'm not judging them or the situation, which creates an additional level of trust. Rarely, there are people who don't open up, and that is totally fine. Again, my job as a reader is to share what I see honestly and give the cards the space to make their move.

## Intuition and the Wisdom of Cards

How to work with your intuition is another question I often get asked. How do you know if your intuition is speaking to you? Have you pulled the right cards? Are you delivering the right message? The best answer for that is simple: Your intuition gets stronger and clearer over time. It simply cannot be rushed or forced.

Just like any sense or muscle you have within your body, the more you use your intuition, the stronger it gets. If you neglect it, it will be weak or dull. If you rely on it, it will get stronger day by day. This is why practice and daily card pulls are so very important.

Practicing listening to your intuition means that you follow the advice of your inner wisdom as often as you can find the strength and bravery to do so. I say *strength* and *bravery* because it can be so hard, and even terrifying, to turn your back on logical reasoning and honor the intuitive voice, especially when its advice or message does not seem to make sense, at least not at first. But again, Spirit sees what we can't and will communicate with us if we ask and are open.

For example, there have been a few times in the middle of a reading when I have felt my throat energetically tighten and close off. I'll go from channeling my messages and spilling them out to my client to suddenly being told by my intuition to completely shut up. The message and images I see for my client are clear to me, and I want to communicate them, and yet my inner wisdom forces me to close my mouth and say no more.

The reality is that I do not see and know all—I am only a messenger for Spirit at the moment. If Spirit asks me to share something specific, I will. If Spirit gives me a vision that is clear, I will also share it. But there are moments when, although I can see what is going to happen next, my client simply isn't meant to. They need to move forward without the information I have, and this is for their own best interest.

The times when I have disobeyed that inner wisdom and shared this information, I have regretted it almost immediately. But I have learned, and now I follow my intuition always. The only reason my intuition, messages, and visions are as sharp as they are now is because I have worked with them and honored them for years. I no longer need to second-guess myself or what I see and feel. This has resulted in better readings for my clients and has also served me in all areas of my life. Whenever I am asked to put aside emotion or logic to tap into an intuitive source, I do it, for I know that it sees more than I do and is working to guide my steps from the mundane to the miraculous. Learn to heed the voice of your intuition, and the same will be true for you.

## Interpreting Cards on the Spot

If you are giving a reading and forget the meaning of the card, don't panic. Remember, you're not on stage or putting on a performance; you're giving a reading. No one should expect you to know all or be all; you are human and are allowed to make mistakes. It happens to the best of us.

It can help to remember that the tarot is as simple as it is complex, and it was designed to trigger your intuitive muscle by the use of symbols, numbers, and colors. If you freeze up during a reading or forget, look at the symbols and images found within the card. Are there certain elements that stand out to you? For example, do you see birds, movement, water, or mountains? Look at the expressions on the faces if there are people represented in the cards. How does that card make you feel? You can ask the querent how it makes them feel so that they are able to connect with the cards and reading even further all on their own!

Sometimes, using your feelings and intuition can be more important than following the rules of the cards. In fact, if you incorporate your intuition into what stands out to you while doing a reading for yourself or your client, you will actually take your reading to the next level.

Remember, the tarot is simply a tool to deliver a message or gift that is stirred up from within you. Allow the cards to speak to you in all the ways they can. Study the meaning of each card, but also pay attention to their symbols and to what personally stands out to you most. Do this, and your reading will truly hit home.

## Making Sense of a Reading on the Spot

There are so many components to a reading—sometimes it can feel like a lot to put all of the pieces together. I'm sure you've heard this many times, but it's so true—practice makes perfect! If you practice, you'll find that it gets easier over time.

When doing a reading, look at each card individually and then step back and look at the greater picture. Is there an appearance of one specific suit? Are there many cards of the Major Arcana? Stepping back and looking at the greater picture will show you the energy around the querent and their question. This helps piece the reading together and gives insight and clarity into what the querent should be receiving from you (or from yourself if you are the querent).

No card is an island, which means that in a spread, they tell a story together: what is happening around the person now, what they can expect, and what is most likely to happen. When you ask the cards a specific question, remember that they are revealing the energy of the question through their answer. But it's also important to remember that, while doing a reading, you are essentially having a conversation with Spirit: If there are areas that stump you, continue the conversation with Spirit by asking for clarity and pulling one more card at any point. This will help you put the whole reading together instead of feeling like you've hit a dead end.

## Spreads and Card Positions

It's pretty tough to give a good reading or understand what the heck is going on if there is no structure or foundation! That's where a designated spread comes in. Spreads are how the cards are literally spread out in order to provide direction and clarity within a reading.

Each position within a spread represents an aspect of what you are asking and creates a firm foundation for the reading. Without a spread, you would have a mess of cards and no direction or help in how to interpret them, which can get confusing quickly!

The number of spreads is pretty much infinite because people are constantly creating new spreads as time goes on and as more are falling in love with the tarot, but there are typical spreads that we tarot readers tend to see or use. For example, the best-known spread is the Celtic Cross, which addresses most aspects that need to be touched on within a reading. It does an

excellent job of creating direction and the "bones" (foundation) of a reading. I use this spread the most and for good reason: No matter the question, it helps me get a clear idea of what is happening around the querent and the question they asked. From there, I usually move on to ask an additional question to keep the conversation between Spirit and me moving forward.

The next spread I use most is the Three-Card Spread: The first card pulled represents the past, the second the present, and the last shows the future or what is to most likely occur if things continue on their current course. Finally, the last most common "spread" is the simplest but still very powerful, the One-Card Pull. You simply ask a question and stay open to what that card is revealing to you. This little spread is best for questions like, "How do they feel about me?" or "What do I need to know before I start my day?" or "When do you see this happening?" In chapter 6, I'll go over these and other spreads in detail.

## Reversals

Whether reversals are included in a reading is a personal choice, and it can vary from reading to reading. I find myself following my intuition and deciding before I start the reading whether or not I will include reversals.

A reversed card is one that appears in the reading upside down, revealing that the energy of the card is blocked or stagnated in some way. Sometimes this can be easily fixed (you can ask your cards how to unblock energy so that it flows again). Other times, reversals can represent major life lessons or opportunities for growth for you or the client (for example, when cards from the Major Arcana appear).

Many readers choose not to work with reversals because they see them as negative. You can go ahead and roll that idea up in a ball and throw it away because this is simply not the case at all. First of all, the tarot's intention is never negative, unless you yourself make it so. Instead, its purpose is to reveal elements to help make you more aware and to support your growth as you make decisions for your own best interest.

Second, a reversed card can actually show that the energy of the card has been opened up or is spilling out, which can be a very good thing! Of course, it all depends on the reading and the context of the question, but don't let your fear of getting negative answers stop you from using reversed cards.

In the chapters on the Major Arcana, Minor Arcana, and Court Cards, I will go into detail about the meaning of each card when reversed and how it applies to the reading. In the meantime, I will leave it to you to

decide if you want to work with them or not. Remember, though, that you don't have to stick with one way or the other indefinitely—you can always change your mind.

While including reversed cards with your tarot reading can provide additional levels of meaning and depth, if you choose not to work with them, there's no reason to feel guilty. If reversed cards appear, you can simply turn them right side up, adjusting the cards in the way that feels most comfortable for you in that moment.

## Delivering Messages Responsibly, Even Bad Ones

There will come a point when you will have to deliver a message that someone doesn't want to hear. Some messages will be heartbreaking. The first thing to realize is that there is no such thing as "bad cards" within the tarot, even ones like The Devil, The Tower, or Death card. We'll dive into the meaning of all of the cards later, but even cards we think would promise positive outcomes don't always represent the things we want to hear. With practice, you will see that reality play out as you learn to look at the bigger picture of the cards, what they are revealing, and how to interpret those messages accurately.

Now, when you come across a message that is difficult for you to accept or digest, you have to remember that all things that happen serve a purpose and that we are here on earth to evolve as much as we can with the time we are given. Some lessons and experiences will be harder to take than others, but you still must be open to them and move through them regardless.

When I see that my client is in a space where they are not going to like the outcome, I ask my spirit guides to provide additional messages of support to help them navigate and steer through this time in their life. No matter the outcome, the reading should always be empowering—that is, the querent receives the truth and the tools to success-fully work with the truth. I never lie or promise things will be anything other than what I see, but I will always provide them with messages from the tarot to help them swim through even the strongest of life's currents.

On the flip side, if you don't like the direction the cards show you are headed in, there are times when you can change the outcome. While the tarot may reveal where you are most likely headed if things continue as they are now, you can also ask the cards what you can do to switch things up to create a future that is more in alignment with what you want for yourself.

Ask the cards to create a plan of action, and they will give you the tools to move forward in a way that leaves you or your client feeling empowered and ready for all that is to come!

## Don't Lie

I cannot stress enough that you should always tell the truth. Some messages simply are not easy to deliver, but they still need to be shared. When you decide that you want to read for others, you are agreeing to take on the good and the bad of what can come from that. Tarot does not always promise rainbows and butterflies, and certain situations can be tough to navigate. Sometimes the reality of what is happening around a client can be shocking. Either way, it is your responsibility to deliver the truth so that they can make the best possible decision for themselves. If you tell them only what they want to hear or share just the aspects of the reading that are the easiest for you to share, you will be letting them walk forward blindly into the lion's den.

However, when telling the truth, remem-ber to be respectful of the way you share your message. Keep in mind that this person is invested in the outcome of what they are asking about, and to burst their bubble in a way that is hurtful or heartless can be harmful. Be compassionate and speak in a way that you would want news broken to you. If necessary, pull a few extra cards that focus on other things they can look forward to, work on, or be excited to see in the near future. There is always room for hope and growth, and you can be the one to give that to them at the end of their reading.

Hopefully, you are starting to see the tremendous power that can be found within the tarot, and you are learning how to wield that sword for yourself and others wisely. Remember that what you put into the cards is exactly what you will get out of them, so continue to practice sharpening your intuitive skills as well as your tarot-reading skills. Understand that delivering difficult messages doesn't have to be negative, and remember the importance of protecting yourself and creating a sacred space for the reading. Let's move on to the next phase where we will explore the meaning of the cards, both reversed and upright.

# PART II
# THE CARDS

# 3

# THE MAJOR ARCANA

**T**HE MAJOR ARCANA COMPRISE 22 CARDS that symbolize major moments or lessons in our lives. Each of the cards blends together symbols, the elements of nature (air, water, fire, and earth), color, and numerology in a way that showcases special moments of personal internal or external transformation. I like to describe the Major Arcana to my students as points on a map indicating must-see experiences and destinations along our life's journey. You may or may not want to go to those "destinations," but when you get there you will learn something about yourself, others, and your environment.

As you study the Major Arcana cards with me in this chapter, pay attention to what we tarot readers like to call "The Fool's Journey." This is the start of the journey with The Fool card, the card of innocence and naivete, the free spirit. As he moves along the road of life (and as you move through each card within the Major Arcana), watch how his experiences shape and change him, ultimately leading him to his final stage of maturity, The World card. Take inspiration from this for your own life, no matter what stage you are in, as you study the tarot.

Now let's dive deep into the meaning of each of the cards of the Major Arcana.

THE FOOL.

"The journey begins with the first step—you may not know what is to come, but you're on your way!"

When The Fool appears within your reading, its message is about faith, fearlessness, and taking the first fresh step in an area of your life. This card's energy is light and unrestricted. Even if there is fear or anxiety, the impulse to start a new phase in your life is too strong to ignore, and you should allow nothing to hold you back. Often this card can suggest a "no strings attached" type of attitude, one free from burdens, attachments, or worry about what the future will hold. Your need to explore and find adventure—to see what else is out there for you—is more powerful than what holds you back. This is a stage in your life to walk out into the unknown!

## Love

There is a need for a fresh start, to be fearless, to move forward with the knowledge that anything can happen. You may be in a space where you don't know where the relationship is headed (maybe it's a new love interest or taking your existing relationship in a new direction), but some kind of shift seems necessary for your growth. In a brand-new relationship where you want a commitment and you see The Fool card, your partner may have a "no strings attached" mind-set; proceed with caution. When this card represents you, it shows a mind-set that needs to move into the unknown, leave the past behind, and start fresh. The appearance of The Fool in a love reading represents trying something new, putting yourself out there.

## Career/Work
The Fool invites you to take risks, step outside of the box, and remove yourself from spaces where you intuitively know you are holding yourself back. It is a card of fearlessness. The Fool understands that bold actions are scary because they trigger change, but a fresh environment and perspective are needed now to support your growth in the working world.

## Personal/Spiritual
Your faith is supported when you fearlessly step into the unknown. The Fool card suggests that you are now in a space where you want to invite new energy into your life. Boldness and faith will be rewarded if you have the courage to take inspired action.

## Reversed
The Fool reversed suggests you are ignoring your own common sense and are possibly engaging in reckless or risky behavior. This is the card's way of saying, "Look before you leap." It's sounding a warning to check yourself before you wreck yourself. At the same time, if you have done your research, and all the signs around you are giving you the green light, The Fool reversed signals that your own hesitation and fear are stopping you from taking the first step. Fear should not control or shape your destiny.

**THE MAGICIAN.**

"You have everything you need to create and manifest your desired outcome now."

Pulling The Magician is an instant reminder of your personal power. Once you have clearly decided what you want to create and attract into your life, this card's appearance is a sign that you have the potential to achieve this desired outcome. *Intention* is the keyword here—what do you want to happen? The Magician is the nudge from the cards calling out the creator in you. Spirit and purpose surge and spark like electricity with this card. Confidence lifts you as you realize that all past challenges have led you to this moment where you alone have the tools, resources, and mind-set to master and influence what will happen next. The Magician is known for his ability to manipulate the elements to master manifestation. Its appearance is a sign that you can make what you have in front of you work for you and for others, if that is what you wish.

## Love

The Magician is one of the most powerful signifiers of soul mates and of using magick or visualization to call in romance or create positive changes within existing relation-ships. It can be a sign that a powerful connection is either on its way or has recently appeared in your life. Sparks will fly when two people come together under the light of The Magician!

## Career/Work

When The Magician appears, you have totally stepped into your personal power! Creative inspiration, word mastery, and focus are working to your benefit. The Magician encourages you to experiment and be assertive and self-assured. Study and practice will yield success. You may be offered an opportunity for public speaking, networking, or to meet a guide who can mentor you at just the right time—take it!

## Personal/Spiritual

On a personal level, The Magician card requires you to believe in yourself and your abilities. Everyone has strengths and weaknesses, but now is the time to focus on your potential rather than on any limiting beliefs or the fear of failure. Spiritually, The Magician works to connect you with the energy of the universe and the Divine. Take this opportunity to use your divinely appointed gifts for your own good and to deepen your spiritual practice through ritual and intention.

## Reversed

When The Magician is reversed, his power is taken from him or blocked. This means you do not believe in yourself, you are not utilizing your skills or tools, or you are waiting for others to tell you what to do instead of making decisions for yourself. Alternately, The Magician reversed can indicate there is someone in your orbit who should not be trusted or that you yourself have ulterior or shady motives.

THE HIGH PRIESTESS

"I have access to a hidden knowledge to help guide me and my next steps forward."

The High Priestess symbolizes listening to and following your intuition, seeking your own inner guidance, looking for deeper meaning, and sometimes taking control to serve your highest interest. The appearance of this card signals that you should quiet yourself and tap into your gut instinct. Be alert to signs and symbols and consider what they are trying to tell you. The High Priestess is connected to hidden information, people, or things, and to access and understand them, you'll need your intuition. If something feels off or wrong, it probably is. The High Priestess will also point you toward someone with access to the spirit world, who has visions, or is highly gifted in working with the subconscious or psychology; this person will provide you with a deeper understanding of the meaning and purpose of your life.

### Love

Even in love readings, The High Priestess signals the need to quiet the mind and listen to your intuition. The High Priestess has everything she needs to make wise decisions, and she is protective of herself and that information. The same should be true for you. Be mindful and aware of the energy around you and that will help you decide what to do next. I've often seen The High Priestess show up for people who need to spend more time with themselves, even if they are in a relationship.

## Career/Work

In career and work, The High Priestess reveals a chance to make use of your unique gifts (especially those revolving around intuition and creativity) to help you along your journey. You may feel drawn to careers involving psychic work, the protection of information or secrets, or maybe even working independently from others without having their input or voice outshine yours. The High Priestess is strong with what she sees and chooses to share, so you may find yourself feeling selective with what you give to others in your work environment or even conserving your energy for other projects or goals.

## Personal/Spiritual

The High Priestess brings confirmation of the intuitive feelings and messages you have been receiving. Meditation, prayer, dreamwork, magick, and setting intentions—all of these will help you deepen your connection to the Divine, your higher self, and to gifts and abilities you never knew existed.

## Reversed

When reversed, The High Priestess's energy is blocked or off balance. Either you are neglecting your own intuition or misusing psychic resources to the point where it has become unhealthy. For example, this card shows up often for people who consult oracles so frequently that they neglect their own feelings. Also, if you know in your gut that something or someone is bad for you but ignore your intuition, The High Priestess will show up reversed and give her last warning.

THE EMPRESS.

"Where you find The Empress is where you will find effortless abundance and growth."

The Empress signals abundance, creativity, and fertility. Her appearance indicates that this is a time that can bring tremendous growth, effortlessly and all on its own. The Empress says, "You have the ability to attract to yourself what you want and need." Be creative, thrive, care, and tend to others as well as yourself. Love, affection, and beauty also go hand in hand with The Empress and are all a part of her magnetism. In my readings, this card has often predicted fertility and pregnancy, especially when pulled with cards like the Ace of Cups, Three of Cups, or Page of Cups. But most often The Empress represents creating and enjoying beautiful moments, slowing down, and receiving the best of life simply because you know you deserve it.

## Love

The Empress signals that love and attraction are growing all on their own. She is a reminder that good things can't be rushed or forced and that your love life will continue to develop as time goes on. Her appearance is a reminder to nurture and take care of the people you love, as well as yourself. Because The Empress represents beauty, she can suggest doing things for yourself that make you feel beautiful to attract what you want. Even in relationships, The Empress never neglects herself and the same should be true for you.

## Career/Work

When The Empress appears, career and work life seem to blossom on their own, the result of all the effort and love you've already invested in achieving your goals. If you are starting a new project or taking on new responsibilities, tend to them daily, without being controlling, to see success build. Timing is everything with The Empress; she understands that development cannot be rushed. But be assured that growth is unfolding and you will reap the rewards if you keep nurturing your work life. Also, be open to receiving assistance (or even asking for it) and not taking everything on yourself.

## Personal/Spiritual

The Empress is a reminder to ease back and receive. Experiencing growth is 50 percent the effort you put in and 50 percent trusting and letting things unfold as they will. Nurture yourself and your needs during this time, realizing that self-care is essential to your personal well-being and health.

## Reversed

The Empress reversed can mean that you are being overly controlling or smothering people around you; you need to take a step back and trust that things will unfold in the way that is best all on their own. This card reversed can also mean you are blocking growth by investing your time, efforts, love, and/or money in the wrong things. The situation may not be conducive to growth at the moment; trying to force it to work may exhaust you.

**THE EMPEROR.**

"I create rules, structure, and stability for myself and others."

The Emperor is emblematic of power, control, and discipline. His appearance is a call to be assertive; it can also be a sign that something is dominating your life—or it could be both. If someone is calling the shots for you, The Emperor can signal the need for you to step into your own personal power and do things for yourself. This card is connected to rational and logical thinking. If there are emotions involved, it is best to control them, since The Emperor comes from a place of power and is not swayed by tears or sob stories. He symbolizes the need for stability, structure, and a plan, especially when it comes to preparing for the future.

## Love

The Emperor's appearance in a love reading is powerful and can represent the need for you to take control of the direction of your love life. If pulled with cards from the Swords suit, it can also mean you are neglecting your own personal feelings and emotions. Establish healthy boundaries between you and the other person, especially if you are the type of person who gives a lot of yourself to others. Be bold and communicate clearly what you want from the relationship, no matter how difficult it might be.

## Career/Work

The Emperor calls on you to embrace and own your power. Create realistic plans and set goals that will ensure you hit important milestones. Be assertive, believe in yourself, and take the initiative in projects you know will be successful.

## Personal/Spiritual

The Emperor is encouraging you to create rules, structure, and stability. To do this, you must use your personal power for your own highest and greatest good. His appearance also indicates the need for establishing healthy personal boundaries, as The Emperor would never allow anyone or anything to disrespect his energy. The same should be true for you.

## Reversed

Reversed, The Emperor's energy is blocked or off balance. Are you trying too hard to assert your will over others or to force something to completion? Is someone trying to dominate you or push their will on you? Or are you neglecting to make decisions out of low self-esteem or holding on to a feeling of powerlessness? Any of these things are destructive to yourself and others. Work on rebalancing your efforts to turn the energy of The Emperor upright again.

**THE HIEROPHANT.**

"I honor the wisdom of tradition."

The Hierophant is about honoring tradition and is representative of the rules and regulations of your own life that provide routine, control, balance, and predictability. They are usually set into place for your protection and to stave off the chaos life can sometimes bring. The Hierophant can connect to the energy of rituals and rites of passage, the church or other religious institutions, established organizations, or educational leaders who are guided to share their knowledge. Its appearance suggests the best course at present may be to maintain the status quo and not rock the boat. Your path should be to follow conventional wisdom or consult an elder or leader if you need guidance.

## Love

The Hierophant can signal that a relationship is moving toward a rite of passage—for example, marriage—or that the relationship is of a traditional or conservative nature in some way. Its appearance can indicate that the love comes more from a sense of responsibility rather than passion or that the relationship could benefit from seeking the guidance of a counselor. For those looking for love, it suggests trying to find love the "old-fashioned" way—that is, waiting for it to happen on its own or asking others to play matchmaker.

## Career/Work

The Hierophant is asking you to consult a trusted advisor to help you develop your future goals. It is not a time to rock the boat; follow the established rules whether or not you agree with them. This card's appearance could also be a suggestion to create more routine in your work schedule.

## Personal/Spiritual

The Hierophant's appearance indicates the need for you to connect with tradition and consult a higher wisdom to give you more clarity. Connecting with a religious or spiritual group may bring greater substance to your own spiritual practice. Also, you may find that consulting the ways of the past by reviewing what others have done before you will help you better understand your present circumstances and provide additional guidance.

## Reversed

Reversed, The Hierophant indicates you're either ignoring traditional wisdom or you've become so rigid in your beliefs that it has become detrimental to your growth. Following rules is good but not to the point that it trumps common sense or intuition.

"I hear the call to make a choice. Which path is the right one for me?"

The Lovers card does not exclusively represent union, although it can sometimes mean two separate things coming together and trying to become one. The main message of The Lovers is actually choice: your power to choose the path you want to take. While this could mean following your heart, never forget that choosing one path means not pursuing another. Whatever you decide, let it be something that resonates completely with you. This card asks you to connect with your heart's truest desires—be honest with yourself and others.

## Love

If you are in a relationship, The Lovers card signals romance, union, sharing, duality, and attraction. But it can also suggest that a decision for the sake of your heart has to be made. Maybe you have to choose between two partners or between your career and a relationship, but there's some type of action you need to explore for your highest and greatest good. Marriage, partnership, engagement, a desire to share your life with another person—all of these things are signaled with The Lovers card.

## Career/Work

The appearance of The Lovers card signifies the need to make an important decision when it comes to your career. You might have to choose between two different job opportunities or reevaluate where your career path is headed.

## Personal/Spiritual

When The Lovers card appears, it's time to assess what it is that your heart truly desires and choose to spiritually align with it. I have seen this card show up in readings to signal the need to set aside time to heal your heart so that you can take a step toward a healthier you.

## Reversed

Reversed, The Lovers can indicate regret in regard to a decision you recently made or the loss of someone or something you truly love and desire. I have also seen this card show up reversed for a person who refuses to follow their heart, choosing instead to make a decision based on logic or others' expectations.

THE CHARIOT.

"Using willpower
and intention, we are
moving forward!"

The Chariot represents purpose, direction, and the clarity of mind necessary to move forward powerfully in your life. This card also connects to transportation and travel, as it often turns up when there is some kind of movement toward a goal or destination. The Chariot symbolizes that you have the power and ability to succeed, to make progress, and to control your environment in order to achieve your goal. With The Chariot, the power of the mind is everything; intention and focus without distraction are the keys to success. If emotions or a foggy mind-set cloud your judgment, your "chariot" can easily tip over.

### Love

The Chariot signifies that you and your partner have (or are working toward) the same goals. If you are single and looking for love, The Chariot shows your desire and intention. If you stay positive and steer clear of distractions, you should find success in love.

## Career/Work

The Chariot indicates you have a strategy for achieving your career goals. This card's appearance may also signify that you will be traveling for work soon or connecting with someone who spends a lot of time on the road.

## Personal/Spiritual

When The Chariot appears, this is a time for you to do everything in your power to maintain a mental space that is clear and focused on the direction of your goal. Because The Chariot deals with travel, you may actually find yourself attending a retreat, going on a vacation with the purpose of rediscovering yourself, or taking a mental health break.

## Reversed

The Chariot reversed means you are unable to move forward. Maybe things are moving too fast, you've lost control, and your "chariot" has tipped over or crashed. Maybe you've lost focus, and you've come to a standstill. Or maybe you're heading in the wrong direction. Whichever it is, your progress forward is now blocked.

"I have the strength to create change without forcing it."

The Strength card usually doesn't represent actual physical strength unless that is what you're asking the cards about. It symbolizes your ability to change an outcome through respect, courage, and patience, and by being gentle—not by force. The Strength card indicates you are facing an obstacle and encourages you to confront whatever it is head-on, even though you may be experiencing fear or anxiety. Communicate your goals and intentions clearly and respectfully, and you will not need force to achieve them.

### Love

Patience and understanding are required now more than ever, as evidenced by the Strength card. You can't force anyone to do your will, and you can't make something happen, no matter how much you want it. Events must spool out organically. The Strength card is a reminder of that. If people sense your good intentions, they are more apt to be open to you. Emotional balance is important to the growth of love for you right now.

## Career/Work

The Strength card indicates that you are using self-discipline and inner confidence to make progress toward your career goals. Internally you may be nervous or afraid, but you're not allowing that to show to others, and they are quickly learning to trust and respect you. Knowing better than to force an issue, you allow things to unfold with gentle nudging and suggestions.

## Personal/Spiritual

The appearance of the Strength card shows that you are stronger than you think you are and that the universe is behind you. You don't need to force things to make them happen. Know what you want and believe that it will manifest. Don't let low self-esteem or negative thinking get the better of you— only you can stop you now.

## Reversed

The Strength card reversed is pointing out that you are trying to force issues instead of allowing them to unfold naturally. This card will appear reversed when you don't trust that something will happen on its own or you try to make it happen. It is telling you that this approach will likely backfire. It can also mean that you are not stepping into your power due to guilt or weakness, or because you would rather have someone else make choices for you.

"I'm searching for answers."

The Hermit is a card of introspection, self-reflection, and going within. Its presence doesn't necessarily suggest that you need to take time to be by yourself, although it's oftentimes needed. The Hermit is searching for answers that may come from within, or it may simply represent a moment in your life where you are focused and doing your own research away from distractions. You may find yourself compelled to pull away from the world to concentrate on your personal goals at this time. The Hermit signifies the need for a deeper level of understanding or a quiet space to retreat.

### Love

In matters of love, the appearance of The Hermit reflects a need for healing or for a pause. You need to withdraw from the world around you for a time to find the answers you need within yourself. This card can also show up if you've been spending a lot of time on your own. And if you are in a loving relationship, it can be a sign that you should concentrate on enjoying each other's company to the exclusion of others for a while.

## Career/Work

The Hermit signifies that you may soon find yourself deeply immersed in a project or engaged in pursuing a work-related goal. This could include examining whether you are truly happy and fulfilled in your current job. The Hermit also counsels patience in these matters. Answers may not be found—or goals achieved—quickly, but that's okay. Seeking the advice of someone you respect or are considering studying with (or who might become a mentor) could help move you closer to your goals.

## Personal/Spiritual

The Hermit suggests that you may need to take time for yourself to disconnect from the day-to-day to find answers to your personal and spiritual questions. You may need to go on a retreat or consult an advisor—including your higher self—to find the clarity you seek.

## Reversed

Reversed, The Hermit may be an indication that you are spending way too much time by yourself, isolated from the rest of the world, to the point where it is detrimental to your well-being. Taking time for yourself can be healing but not if you are using it to escape your responsibilities or avoid things you know you should do. The company of others will lift your spirits and bring light back into your life.

**WHEEL of FORTUNE.**

"Fate has stepped in and is divinely guiding you."

The Wheel of Fortune is a card of changing events. It represents the cycles of time. Nothing is permanent; even the highs and the lows are temporary, constantly changing as life moves forward. Oftentimes, this card signifies good luck and a change for the better—things developing in a way that feels progressive or fortunate. The Wheel of Fortune represents a move from one phase of your life into the next.

## Love

In love readings, the Wheel of Fortune brings good luck and movement forward! This card is very similar to astrology charts and is a reminder that some things are destined to occur in your life according to divine timing. Changes around you now seem to be for the better and bring in good luck and opportunities. You may also feel like luck just happens to be on your side and that you strike gold in your love relationships.

## Career/Work

The Wheel of Fortune forecasts the likelihood of opportunities, accomplishment, and success. Circumstances around your work environment are changing for the better. You may meet someone at the right place at the right time who can advance your career or offer you an opportunity, and you may achieve your work goals faster than you originally thought.

## Personal/Spiritual

The Wheel of Fortune reminds us of the importance of fate, but also that nothing is truly forever. The wheel of life, as represented by this card, is constantly moving. Whether you are in a slump or at a high point, understand that it is temporary and can only be experienced in that moment. The Wheel of Fortune brings with it feelings of luck— new chapters may be opening in your life that you will be grateful for.

## Reversed

When reversed, the Wheel of Fortune can't move forward; its energy is blocked in some way. You may be feeling unlucky or like your efforts aren't paying off the way you think they should. You could be disappointed with something or feeling like your life has taken a turn for the worse. Still, the message of the card remains the same as when upright: Nothing is permanent and everything changes, so whatever state you're currently in, it is temporary. The wheel of life will turn for good once more.

**JUSTICE.**

"All will be taken into consideration and will be handled for the fairest and most just outcome."

Justice shows up when you are considering the pros and the cons of a particular action in your life. This card represents moderation, fairness, and balance. Justice is unemotional in order to find the truth of the matter and arrive at a fair outcome. Its appearance means that someone is trying to make the right decision in regard to something, and they are considering all the sides. It could be that you are engaged in a legal battle. If you are in the right, Justice signifies the outcome will be in your favor. If, however, you are at fault, you will receive a punishment that fits the crime. The Justice card represents the energy around you determining what your punishment or reward should be.

## Love
When Justice appears, you seem to be weighing the pros and cons of a possible relationship or the state of your love life right now. Put your emotions on the back burner in order to come up with a decision that will benefit you and/or your partner. Sometimes the Justice card can mean there is a mismatch between how much you are giving and how much you are receiving. For your relationship to thrive, there must be balance between the two.

## Career/Work

The Justice card advises caution in work matters at this time. It could be you are weighing the pros and cons of a career opportunity or that you feel the need to find balance in your work life to stay productive. This card's appearance could also mean that your work is being critiqued.

## Personal/Spiritual

When Justice appears in your personal reading, it is a call to emotionally distance yourself so you can make a fair and just decision for your highest and greatest good. Maybe you are too invested in an outcome, and you need to take a step back. Or maybe you need to let someone else carry the burdens of responsibility if they have fallen heavy on your shoulders (or maybe you need to carry them for someone else). Justice wants what is fair for everyone, but especially what is fair and just for you.

## Reversed

Justice reversed signifies injustice. It can seem like someone is "getting away with murder" or escaping punishment in some way. I've seen this card show up in a reading of someone wrongly accused. It can also mean that your judgment is currently being guided too much by emotion to the neglect of logic and reason. Justice reversed reminds you to not be too soft or emotionally swayed by others, or they may feel free to overstep their boundaries or take advantage of you and your kindness.

THE HANGED MAN.

"I can't fight or force the things that I cannot control. For this reason, I surrender."

The Hanged Man represents total release and surrender to circumstances outside your control. The universe has brought you to a point where you are hanging in limbo, and there is no good move you can make for the time being. Something has you in a space where you are in total suspension, and, in most cases, fighting it will create more harm than good. The Hanged Man signals this is a time to let go, trust, and release your will to the unknown. Although this may be a good time to try seeing things from a totally different perspective, it's very possible that the best thing to do now is absolutely nothing.

### Love

The Hanged Man indicates that you are in a state of limbo; there is no movement forward or backward—you're just hanging around, waiting in suspension and suspense. You may need to abandon any expectations for the relationship temporarily at this time—pause and not force or rush anything. If you are ready to move forward with a relationship, The Hanged Man could indicate that your partner may not have the same idea or that you are fearful of speaking the truth from your heart. For singles, it may seem like there is no progress in your dating life—or at least not the kind you may have been hoping for. This card reminds you to trust that the universe is holding you in good hands and doesn't want you to move forward for a reason. Let go of your need to control.

## Career/Work

The Hanged Man symbolizes feelings of powerlessness regarding your work situation. You may find yourself waiting for a message or for something to materialize. This card can also suggest letting go of your need to control, instead being more open to taking direction from others and hearing different points of view.

## Personal/Spiritual

The Hanged Man in personal readings is incredibly powerful because it shows that learning to let go and trust in something bigger than yourself will lead to your highest and greatest good. Trusting in these forces may seem like surrender, but you are, in fact, allowing yourself to be picked up and guided toward what you need with perfect divine timing. This card reminds you to have faith in yourself and the universe. Believe it or not, it is possible to enjoy this limbo phase if you relax into it and know that this will make the progress that much faster!

## Reversed

When reversed, The Hanged Man shows that you are struggling to maintain control, refusing to let go to the point where it has become a detriment to your well-being. You may be fighting the inevitable or refusing to see things for what they are out of fear or a resistance to moving forward into the future. On the other hand, this card can signify that you may be staying in a space of helplessness and making yourself a victim.

"I'm experiencing a period of incredible transformation!"

Death is the card of total and complete transformation. It is one of my favorites within the Major Arcana because when this card appears, it reveals that the circumstances around you have entered into a cycle of purging, cleansing, and releasing. Something around you now is coming to completion to make room for new growth. Wherever there is an ending, there is always a beginning, and the Death card is a symbolic representation of that process occurring in your life now. With any kind of "death," that energy is born anew in some other form. You may be releasing toxic people, thoughts, or things; moving from one place to the next; or saying goodbye to someone or something for now.

## Love

The Death card symbolizes the end of some aspect of the relationship. Your love life is totally changing and revamping itself. It's possible that this can bring feelings of sadness, but at the same time, I have seen this card (very often!) show up for people who were moving from one phase of love to another or saying goodbye to singledom and welcoming love into their lives.

## Career/Work

Your career and work life are under a spell of transformation when the Death card shows up. Something is coming to an end and the universe is preparing you for a new beginning. This card is a wonderful sign if you have been setting intentions to create a major change in your life, but if you are to be laid off from your job, it can definitely bring disappointment, too. Either way, you are reaching an end, experiencing a cut of some sort and being asked to be flexible as this transformation takes place.

## Personal/Spiritual

You are laying to rest aspects of your life that no longer serve you, as indicated by the Death card. You may be forced out of a situation or find yourself in the midst of a total transformation as parts of your life melt away and take on a new form. With Death, it's important to remain open to these changes, even if they seem to your detriment initially.

## Reversed

When reversed, the Death card can signify that you are avoiding necessary change. You may be holding on to something or grieving to the point where you have stopped experiencing the magick of your own life. Remember, every ending is the beginning of a new journey that will bring gifts all of its own. Resisting change doesn't stop it from happening, but it can and will **prolong suffering**.

TEMPERANCE.

"I am working to bring opposite energies together to create something new."

Temperance signifies that this is a major moment to bring balance, moderation, and alchemy into your life. This card represents taking two very separate and different things and bringing them together to create some new form. This requires trial and error, which is why this card also symbolizes patience. Balance is needed, but in the eyes of the Temperance card, balance doesn't have to be a 50/50 split. It means finding the right mix of elements that works for you or helps you meet your goal. These two elements can be two people from different backgrounds or with different lifestyles. Either way, the appearance of the Temperance card means they are now working to come together in a magical new form in a way that's best for them.

## Love

Temperance is about two people trying to figure out how to merge together. It represents patience but also respect for each other's differences, including finding out what works best for you both. You may be experimenting with different ways of communicating or working your schedules to make time for each other. If you are single, it may signify that you need to be patient with the universe as it works to find your "better half" for you. Take your time, the Temperance card says—don't try to rush to work things out. Patience is needed now more than ever, as well as understanding and an open mind.

## Career/Work

When Temperance appears, you are trying to find balance or a system that works for you at your workplace. You may be trying out ideas, trying on new roles, or working with totally different groups of people to bring a project or goal to completion. Because there are so many different variables involved, you want to make room for some trial and error and not expect perfection right out of the gate. If you learn more about the project or the people involved with it, you will find you have a better shot at moving forward and creating something special and unique. Remember, patience is always needed with the Temperance card, no matter the question asked.

## Personal/Spiritual

The Temperance card signals a need for moderation and balance. Where in your life does there seem to be too much or too little? Now is the time to rework this chemistry in a way that makes you feel better and supports your ability to thrive, not just survive. This card gives you permission to slow down, forgive yourself and others, and take it easy.

You can also find yourself working out a balance within yourself—between your shadow side and light side—or trying to find where you fit in the world and who or what belongs beside you.

## Reversed

When reversed, the Temperance card is symbolic of some kind of extreme. Balance is lost—there is either too much or not enough of something. We see this card when we are overindulging, worn down and not resting, or forcing an issue. Also, sometimes two different things are not destined to come together or to work, at least not now. Reversed, this card suggests that the differences are just too great to blend successfully. Find something else or pause to restore order once more.

THE DEVIL.

"I'm exploring temptation, addiction, and attachments."

The Devil represents bonds, commitment, temptation, and vices. There are two sides to The Devil card—the good and the bad—and both show up, no matter whether the card is upright or reversed. Let's start with the good: When The Devil appears in a positive reading, it represents making commitments (for example, a wedding or signing an important business contract). This tie should be lasting and binding, not something you can easily break, and it is very much a good thing. The Devil can also remind you to enjoy life's pleasures (for example, a slice of chocolate cake after a long detox diet) and the satisfaction and reward you feel in the tiny indulgence that you worked hard for. In negative readings, this card can signify unhealthy bonds or addictions, toxic or damaging temptation (for example, infidelity), or unhealthy patterns of thinking.

## Love

In love readings, when The Devil appears, it's very important to look at the surrounding cards or pull a clarifying card if you're not sure what this card is suggesting. It can represent temptation, attachment, passion, and commitment to a relationship in a way that is positive, or it can hint that obsession, cheating, or unhealthy behaviors are manifesting. If you are prone to worst-case-scenario thinking, The Devil card could be flagging this tendency as your biggest enemy. I have seen this card show up many times in relationship readings where one person is obsessed that their worst fears will be realized, which ends up sabotaging the entire relationship.

## Career/Work

When The Devil appears in a career reading, you may be signing a binding contract or making an agreement that feels heavy or permanent. Sometimes this card appears when you feel like a slave to your job to the point where it's almost impossible to have a personal life. Other times, The Devil's appearance can show a working environment that is toxic, draining, or simply uncomfortable to be in, but you couldn't change it or leave it if you tried at this time.

## Personal/Spiritual

The Devil's appearance asks you to examine who or what the "devil" is in your life right now. If it is negative thinking, an unhealthy obsession, or toxic behavior or commitments, then it is time for you to cut them loose. However, this card can be a reminder to not be so hard on yourself, that life is meant to be both experienced and enjoyed. Treating yourself occasionally will not harm you, and sometimes rebelling a little against what you are supposed to do is good for the soul. The Devil is very stubborn, and this card can signify that you're having a hard time letting go; you might want to consider seeking support or treatment to keep bad behaviors at bay.

## Reversed

The Devil reversed brings equal "good" and "bad" with it. Again, let's start with the good: You have finally decided to free yourself from ties that have been holding you back. You are feeling free, unrestrained, even limitless! You may have faced some fears, conquered demons, and cut toxic cords. You might also be celebrating your newfound freedom (for example, you've gotten divorced or have broken out of an unhappy situation). The negatives? Well, those old demons can continue to linger or even regain control. It can feel almost impossible to be in control or to contain an obsession or maintain your freedom. Again, these cords are stubborn and difficult to break on your own. I usually encourage my clients to get additional help; it can be too much for one person to handle.

THE TOWER.

"Drastic developments are happening, and I expect the unexpected."

The Tower represents total shock, surprise, breakthrough—an unexpected development. This card will always show up when something unseen is in the works, and when it reveals itself, it will take your breath away because you never saw it coming. It's a total departure from the normal, a deviation from your usual. I have seen this card represent shakedowns and eye-opening revelations as well as moments that changed the course of a client's life forever. It's really important when this card shows up that you don't panic and that you remain flexible and open. The universe has a way of always keeping us on our toes with surprises, but every once in a while, we get hints and signs of what is to come. When The Tower card shows up in a reading, this is your sign!

## Love

The Tower can bring news of surprise engagements (if you are waiting for a ring, should I even be telling you this? How will it ever be a surprise, then?), breakthrough moments, and maybe even breakups. Or maybe your partner confesses a truth they've been holding in their heart for a while. Whatever the news, usually, it will catch you off guard. You will definitely be experiencing some kind of revelatory moment that will change the dynamic of the relationship for good or bad. This is something that you cannot force; it will happen all on its own, so stay open.

## Career/Work

When The Tower appears, you will experience an unexpected change in your workplace. It could be positive, like a surge of orders, an exciting new client, or a project that inspires creativity. But it could include bad news—getting fired, the business seeming to fall apart overnight, or some kind of shocking revelation. Or maybe you are the one who is kicking up dust by deciding to quit. Whatever the change, it tends to be something that has been in the works for a while, but I have also seen it be utterly random, hence the surprise of it all.

## Personal/Spiritual

The appearance of The Tower suggests that there is a breakdown, collapse, or major life-changing moment in store for you. It will take you by surprise, even if it is you who is pulling the plug on things in a way that people would never expect you to. In fact, The Tower could be encouraging you to make a radical change that will fuel your personal growth. Even if it seems out of the blue, you'll find this change has been percolating for quite a long time and is just now coming to fruition.

## Reversed

When reversed, The Tower can show that circumstances or timing helped you narrowly escape some major drastic disruption in your life. Because this card rules the element of surprise, it can seem almost impossible to predict what will happen reversed or upright! Either way, it will show up when something shocking is about to occur and lessen the intensity of the surprise.

**THE STAR.**

"I find hope, healing, and inspiration around me now."

The Star always brings hope, healing, and inspiration in any reading, whether it appears upright or reversed. It reminds you that, even in the darkest of times, you should keep the faith and look for guidance, and you will be held in protection as you move toward a brighter future. For centuries, people have used the stars to guide them in the major decisions of their life or to act as a compass as they travel into the unknown. The Star encourages you to look for the signs, consult astrology charts, or even simply ask for directions. Because this card is about having hope, I often see it appear for clients experiencing darker moments, when things seem hopeless. The Star is confirmation that this isn't the end of the road yet—there is more to come for you in the future!

## Love

The Star always brings hope, healing, and good fortune when it appears, but especially so in a love reading. Some aspect of your love life is being worked on or healed in a way that will feel very positive. If you and your partner are struggling or you are single and losing hope that you'll find love, this card reminds you not to give up. Timing is key, and you may need to have faith in the Divine.

This cannot be rushed or planned. It just has to happen. Speak words of love, light, and healing, and you can really experience profound change overnight.

## Career/Work

In work-related matters, The Star is not just a symbol of hope; it is a sign that something good is waiting for you just over the horizon, especially when it comes to creative fields of study, healing, communication, or entertainment. This is that moment when your dreams can come true if you can match the stars in your eyes with effort. If you were thinking about giving up on your dream or feel like you are losing the energy to move forward, The Star gives you permission to take a break, but counsels you not to give up. There is something important brewing in the stars for you, but you need to keep moving toward it to receive it.

## Personal/Spiritual

Healing is abundant now—spiritually, mentally, physically. The appearance of The Star signifies that miracles are possible; ask for what you need and want and believe it can happen. Prayer, meditation, and setting intentions seem important to you now. If not, it may be that you need to take time to focus on your spiritual self and healing and ask for guidance from the Divine.

## Reversed

Even when reversed, The Star brings positive messages. You may simply be lacking hope now or wondering if things will truly pan out as you desire. The Star reversed may be indicating that you need a little boost to believe that miracles are possible. It is okay to ask for help. Look for inspiration and ask for clarification. Also, focus on healing and restoring yourself so you can feel strong again.

**THE MOON.**

"I'm learning that nothing is what it seems."

The Moon card is one of the most complex and confusing in the deck because that is exactly what it represents! When The Moon appears, circumstances and people around you tend to not be what they seem to be; there are elements of confusion, with things seeming either worse or better than they actually are. This card represents fantasy, illusion, fear, the things we hide or can't clearly see or understand, and sometimes simply the energy of the moon herself. That energy is primal, raw, and forever changing; you cannot rely on it or predict it. I have seen this card show up in a reading to signal that someone is being lied to, but also when someone is letting their imagination run away with them, for good or for bad.

## Love

The Moon card asks, "Can you really trust this person, their actions, or their words?" If things don't feel right or seem off, they probably are. It could also be that you see someone in a light that makes them appear better than they are. But the flip side is that you don't want to go looking for shadows where there are none; if you expect the worst, it could be self-fulfilling.

## Career/Work

If you are pursuing a career in psychology, the arts, or therapy, The Moon can be a nod toward that in a work-related reading. Otherwise, it shows up when things around you seem to be in a constant state of flux, your work environment is unpredictable, or you are getting bogged down by stress and pressure to the point that it is negatively affecting your mental health. The Moon also may be signaling to you that someone is behind the scenes trying secretly to sabotage you, your work, and your reputation.

## Personal/Spiritual

When The Moon appears, I always have to question if I or my client is seeing things accurately for what they really are. It may not be on purpose, but when The Moon appears, something is not right. This card is a suggestion to check your environment—and yourself—and to not make any assumptions. You may feel confused or foggy, or be unclear about your direction, so no moves should be made at this time. Also, moods tend to rise and fall and change quickly, where one minute's feeling can create a whirlwind of change you may later regret. Wait for things to become clearer before proceeding.

## Reversed

The Moon reversed heightens the illusion to the next level, cranking it up to 100 percent. This is problematic because not only can you still not see something for what it truly is, but now you are also refusing to step into the light and face reality. This form of escapism can be destructive, especially if it involves drugs, alcohol, or active deception. You may finally discover who your enemy is and how they have been working against you all this time.

THE SUN.

"I'm entering into a time of great joy, happiness, and success in my life!"

The Sun brings joy, abundance, good vibes, and warm feelings all around. Usually when it appears, The Sun signifies the receipt of good news or indicates that you are facing obstacles with a positive attitude and spirit, which is helping move things forward for the better. I find this card shows up when people are celebrating, have achieved a major milestone, or have found a space of pure peace within themselves. The card is about sharing and even feeling good in the company of others, so oftentimes it shows up when you are surrounded by friends and family. Children or people with youthful spirits tend to surface when this card appears because they bring with them joy and a sense of free spirit.

## Love

The Sun is an excellent card to receive in a love reading. It brings joy, optimism, laughter, fun, and play: important qualities to attract and bring into a relationship. Because this card is filled with so much positive energy, it can show a date that goes exceedingly well, marriage, or a moment together that makes you feel on top of the world! If you're single and looking for love, you'll benefit from going out, celebrating, and mingling because the chances of meeting someone are higher than usual, and you'll enjoy yourself in the meantime. Having a smile on your face as well as warm energy makes you naturally attractive, and using the power of positive thinking will make the success you visualized manifest in your love life.

## Career/Work

In work-related readings, The Sun brings happiness, success, fulfillment, and encouragement. You might be receiving a reward or recognition for your efforts. Work seems to be fun or at least fulfilling at this time. Your focus is high, people want to work with you, your ego is getting (positively) inflated, and your reputation seems to be well regarded. However, I have seen this card sometimes show up for people who seem to always be goofing off, which can be detrimental to their professional growth.

## Personal/Spiritual

The Sun indicates a time to look on the bright side, think positively, and concentrate on what is working in your life. Make time for joy, family, and friends; get out and circulate; and engage in activities for the sole purpose of putting a smile on your face. Health and happiness are yours now and seem to take center stage as you focus on increasing your vitality. Positive thinking can change outcomes, and you are experiencing that now. Also, you may be seeing the light of hope and faith within the spiritual side of yourself.

## Reversed

Even reversed, The Sun is positive and brings good news. The light is still there; it's just that you may not be able to see it and feel it now. Success may be a little late, but that doesn't mean it isn't coming. Or maybe you are on the tail end of celebrations and feeling pleasantly exhausted from the festivities and fun. Relaxation might be on your mind now; allow your body time to recharge.

JUDGEMENT.

"I am leaving one phase of my life and entering into the next, completely reborn!"

Judgement shows up when you are experiencing major revelations, changes, and milestones in your life. Maybe the consequences of past actions are rearing their head now, maybe you are receiving some kind of wake-up call, or maybe there is a new chapter bursting open in your life after a long wait. Whichever it is, something is bubbling up to the surface. This card represents the truth—seeing people and things for what they are. This revelation is eye opening and life changing and will affect how you decide to move forward. You can't hide things under the rug anymore because the rug has been ripped up and all is being revealed. A new door is opening, and, for many, this will feel like a total rebirth.

## Love

In love readings, the Judgement card can be intense but necessary. You have realized that there are aspects of yourself or others that need to change, or maybe you have realized that some things will always stay the same, which can be equally healing, whether it disappoints or enlightens. There is some kind of major change in store for you that will shake you to your core but is needed. You will finally know what it is that you need to do; be brave and make the first move.

## Career/Work

The Judgement card indicates that huge revelations and changes are happening around you now. This card shows up when you realize something new about yourself or the work you've been doing. Perhaps you have a sudden need for a career change or change in purpose. I have also seen this card show up for people who are feeling judged or called out in some way, perhaps from past mistakes or decisions. When the Judgement card appears, it is like hearing a trumpet blow—it is never, ever subtle. You may also be experiencing some kind of rebirth in your work environment.

## Personal/Spiritual

Who you thought you were or what you thought you wanted may be called into question now, as indicated by the Judgement card. A growth cycle is ending in your life, but with that comes rebirth and, more important, awareness. You are wiping the slate clean and starting over fresh with a new version of who you are now (we are forever changing)! The Judgement card requires that you see yourself and your surroundings for what they are; avoid the trap of trying to sugarcoat reality, even though it might make you feel better. The easy way out is not always the best.

## Reversed

Judgement reversed means you are refusing to see things for what they are and trying to hold on to the status quo. You may be forced to move forward even though you don't feel ready. If you had your way, everything would stay the same forever, but the universe doesn't see it that way. Growth can seem really difficult at this time as can accepting the truth of your reality, but it needs to be done.

"Finally, I've reached the final stage. Success!"

The World is the card of completion, signifying that a cycle is ending and you are moving on to the next phase of your life. In some way, you are being called upon to graduate, to take all the lessons you learned and apply them in a way that will build a constructive path to your future. For many, this card shows up with a feeling of accomplishment and completion. You've worked so hard and now you are seeing the fruits of all those efforts. But it can also be accompanied by a feeling of sadness, as you are saying goodbye to an old stage or phase. That's natural, but remember that new opportunities await you—the world is literally calling to you now!

## Love

The World symbolizes the end of one cycle and movement toward the next. You might be moving from being engaged to being married or from being in a relationship to being single. Whatever it is, you are heading into a new phase. This card doesn't usually appear in a new relationship unless your potential partner expands your view of the world or there is a lot of travel involved for the two of you.

## Career/Work

The World signifies success and accomplishment. You may be finally seeing the reward after all the hard work you've been putting in. It may signal a graduation or a promotion. Whatever it is, you've earned it! You've discovered how to take everything you've learned from your experiences and apply it to master a goal. Because The World card connects to international dealings, you may also find yourself traveling or working with clients all over the world.

## Personal/Spiritual

The World shows that you are making huge strides toward your goals for self-improvement, personal success, and accomplishment. This varies for everyone because we each have different things we aspire to be, achieve, or feel, but there is sure to be a sense of reward for the hard work you have been putting in toward self-improvement. You are focused on growth, ending one cycle of your life to begin the next. The effort is paying off now!

## Reversed

Reversed, The World suggests that you are having a difficult time entering into this new phase of your life and trusting in the journey. You may feel you are not ready or are struggling to say goodbye to one stage and move on the next. When The World card shows up reversed, it is saying that you are in fact ready—just believe in yourself!

# 4

## THE MINOR ARCANA

**T**HE CARDS OF THE MINOR ARCANA REPRESENT every aspect of our daily lives—from the dull and mundane (lookin' at you, Four of Cups) to the cold slap of reality (this one is for you, Ace of Swords) to the feeling of flying (Six of Wands, this is your moment)! While the Major Arcana reflect major milestones of your life, the Minor Arcana are wrapped up in all the aspects you can see and feel in this moment. They paint a more detailed picture of what is revolving around the question you've asked. You'll look into people's trails, mind-sets, ideas, and activities while working with these cards.

The Minor Arcana are broken down into four suits: Cups, Wands, Swords, and Pentacles. Each of these brings totally different energy to bear and is representative of a set of astrological signs. You'll also see that numerology plays an important role as you move through each suit from Ace to Ten. Let's look at each in turn.

# CUPS

**ASTROLOGICAL SIGNS:**
Pisces, Cancer, Scorpio

**ELEMENT:**
Water

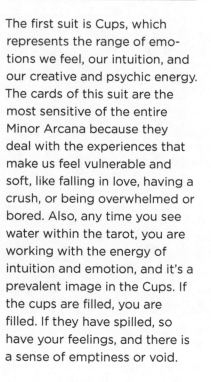

The first suit is Cups, which represents the range of emotions we feel, our intuition, and our creative and psychic energy. The cards of this suit are the most sensitive of the entire Minor Arcana because they deal with the experiences that make us feel vulnerable and soft, like falling in love, having a crush, or being overwhelmed or bored. Also, any time you see water within the tarot, you are working with the energy of intuition and emotion, and it's a prevalent image in the Cups. If the cups are filled, you are filled. If they have spilled, so have your feelings, and there is a sense of emptiness or void.

# ACE OF CUPS

ACE of CUPS.

*"My heart bursts with love, emotions, and color and I can barely contain myself!"*

The Ace of Cups corresponds to the bubbling up of pure emotion. This card points to those moments in your life where you feel butterflies and your inspiration soars. You not only see color, but it's also like you can taste it—*that's* how magical this card is! Because this card is the first in the suit, it is showing you that a new beginning is imminent—a door has opened to your heart. It can feel almost impossible to swallow all these feelings that are bubbling up. Imagine a fountain in the center of a beautiful park. Picture the people, birds, and butterflies gravitating toward it, attracted to its beauty and the action of the water. This is the same energy that the Ace of Cups is bringing to you when it appears in your spread.

## Love

The Ace of Cups is a card of magick and beauty all by itself! In love readings, it may represent falling in deep, head over heels for someone—or someone else feeling this way for you. Your heart has totally opened, and the emotions there are swelling and swirling within you. New love may enter your life, or an established relationship may grow and thrive. You may hear soft, intimate words of affection and attraction—what will you do with them?

## Career/Work

The Ace of Cups shows up a lot in career readings when your creativity takes center stage. Because the Ace of Cups connects with emotion and feeling, you are called to place your logical reasoning aside and give your creative, imaginative brain a chance to play. Remember, the Aces signify the start of some new venture. You may find yourself considering a new offer or proposal in your work environment very soon.

## Personal/Spiritual

Your heart's healing and its authentic expression are the key messages when the Ace of Cups appears. For starters, this card is teaching you the importance of building a healthy connection with your intuition, your emotions, and your creative self. You may be asked to consider whether you are truly happy and, if not, to prioritize your pursuit of joy, love, and balance. You may be called to

listen to your heart for deeper guidance to fill your cup of life all the way up!

## Reversed

Reversed, the Ace of Cups represents a totally drained vessel. Maybe someone or something has knocked it over and what spills out is disappointment, unrequited feelings, sadness, or frustration. Maybe you are the one who refuses to express your heart's truest message, so it feels dried out and forgotten. Consider asking yourself, "What can I do to turn this cup around so that I can be filled and bubbling with life once more?"

## TWO OF CUPS

"I choose you. You and I are coming together. Wonderful things await us, and together we will build!"

The Two of Cups can show you the moment you find your other half—something that's been missing in your life. Sometimes this will manifest as a person, but I have also seen this show up as a new work partnership, a fresh alliance, or a place—a living space or community—that immediately feels like home. At its core, this card equates to mutual attraction and partnership. It is the card of two separate, imperfect entities seeing the perfection in choosing each other. The mutual sharing that flows between them makes the partnership feel effortless and inevitable.

## Love

In love, the Two of Cups suggests that you have found your other half and are interested in coming together as one. Oftentimes, people assume that the appearance of the Two of Cups means this bond should and will be forever, but it only promises union and partnership—it doesn't imply a length of time. Both people will feel attraction, you will share giving and receiving equally, and it can feel as though the stars aligned to bring you together. You may have moved beyond the initial "relationship talk," as this card is showing you that you are cementing and creating something tangible from your feelings for each other.

## Career/Work

The Two of Cups shows that you are joining forces with a business partner or collaborator or are linking with another business.

Your collaborators have seen the potential in you and in a partnership with you. As a team, you are working to see what you can build and create together. It's important to communicate clearly about expectations and to fully disclose your wishes and goals for the partnership. These practices will help create a firm foundation for this new venture. The commonly seen figures on the Two of Cups card both present their cups as offerings and hold nothing back—this kind of openness and generosity is what it will take to make this relationship work. Both parties have something to gain from each other.

## Personal/Spiritual

The Two of Cups suggests that this is the time to examine your alliances and partnerships. Maybe you are even in a place in your life where you feel so filled up that it seems only natural for you to share that wealth of good vibes and love with others around you! The universe works to find balance, so it may be quick to complement your energy of generosity and fullness by bringing your "other half" into your life. When this card appears, it may mean that you are aligning with the energy of "the other" and that you will both learn through your experiences together.

## Reversed

When the Two of Cups is reversed, the energy of a partnership and union is fractured or broken. It may seem as though the connection between you and someone else—whether a romantic partner, a friend, or a colleague—is "off" or out of balance, so now the bond between you has suffered. This card often shows up reversed when you are giving a lot of yourself and may be receiving little to nothing in return.

## THREE OF CUPS

"There is so much here that we have to celebrate! Let's use this time to enjoy the moment!"

The Three of Cups is the card of partying, drinking and eating, and having a good time! This card illustrates stages in your life where you are celebrating. You may find yourself out circulating, mixing and mingling, or going to clubs, parties, or bars—places created for having a good time and letting your hair down. Even if the card doesn't represent an actual party or outing, it may indicate people who lift you up, root for you, and support you. They don't have to be physically near you to be celebrating and encouraging you! You may find yourself in a space where you acknowledge your own growth and accomplishments.

## Love

In love readings, the Three of Cups can be pretty tricky. As wonderful as this card may seem, I have very often seen it show up in a spread to represent love triangles or a third-party type of situation. If you are experiencing boredom or problems in your relationship, this card may suggest that an outside person or influence might be involved that is more entertaining—to you or your partner—than your relationship with each other. If you see this card in a spread, I suggest you keep your third eye, your intuition, open for that. On the flip side, in relatively happy partnerships, this card can appear when you have people around who are cheering your love life on. And if you're not in a relationship at the moment, it can signify lots of new relationship opportunities.

## Career/Work

In work-related readings where the Three of Cups appears, the symbolism of the number 3 can be literal: It might symbolize that three entities could be joining forces to work together in a successful collaboration. Or it may represent you taking time to celebrate some major achievements in your office or networking with coworkers outside your usual working hours. This card tends to bring fun distractions and lifted spirits as people let loose and enjoy themselves and each other for a few hours. This card shows up a lot for those who are interested in networking and building alliances in creative ways; usually the payoff tends to be excellent for businesses of all kinds!

### Personal/Spiritual

The universe is all about balance, including the balance between work and play. When the Three of Cups appears in a reading, it's a great cosmic nudge to stop and celebrate the beauty of this moment. Allow others the chance to be there to support you and show how much they care! This card reminds you that life is not meant to be heavy or serious all the time, and it encourages you to let yourself relax and find things that bring you pleasure with the people who make you smile. It's a reminder that joy and fun are just as important as hitting your personal-growth goals. Make time for both.

### Reversed

The Three of Cups reversed means the party and celebrations have been canceled or maybe that they have gone on for too long. This card reversed can point to excess—maybe too much drinking or partying. This is when "having a good time" goes wrong. It can bring the energy of regret, hangovers, sadness, or disappointment. And remember how I mentioned earlier that the Three of Cups can represent a third party in relationships? Well, this card may show up reversed when this other person has been found out; there are feelings not only of regret but also of remorse.

## FOUR OF CUPS

"I am not interested in what you are offering."

The Four of Cups can bring two very different types of messages. It either stands for your boredom or shows that what you currently have is all you want and you are not open to anything more. Regardless of which way this message swings for you, the energy around you will remain stubborn and unmoving because that is the nature of the number 4's symbolism, always. In the traditional Rider-Waite deck, you can see the person's face is unamused and unmoving—he is not unfolding his arms to accept what is being handed to him. If you are working with a deck other than the Rider-Waite, the imagery might change but the meaning behind it stays the same. The interpretation depends on whether you are the person who is extending the offering or the one who is refusing to receive it.

### Love

There are two sides to the coin when the Four of Cups appears. You may find yourself either bored in your current relationship or simply not open to changing the status quo—whatever that is—because what you have now is enough. This card usually does not symbolize satisfaction, however. Remember, the suit of Cups represents emotions. With the Four, these feelings can be boredom, lack, or dissatisfaction. Maybe you are involved in a relationship not out of love but out of obligation. You may be going through the motions in your romantic partnership but not feeling called and inspired. If you are single, this card shows up when your dating options are not making you happy or you are bored by the way your love life is unfolding.

### Career/Work

The Four of Cups symbolizes total boredom and dissatisfaction revolving around the question you've asked. Maybe you have received a job offer, but something about the offer is off-putting to you. Perhaps the pay is not enough or maybe the employer is asking you to relocate, though your current location feels like home. This is a chance to dig more deeply into the areas of your career that you don't like and to identify what is missing or lacking for you.

### Personal/Spiritual

The Four of Cups is showing you that you are in a space where you want and need more for yourself. You might be in a place where certain areas of your life need an overhaul; they're just not serving you in the same way anymore. You may be realizing that you don't have to say yes to everything asked of you, especially if it doesn't spark passion for you. Only you know the answer to what will bring you joy and fill you up—whether that be an exciting adventure, a relaxing vacation, or a totally different belief system or philosophy.

### Reversed

Four of Cups reversed symbolizes revisiting an old decision that has been made: "I've changed my mind . . . I may say yes now . . . ." This card reversed shows you that someone in your life has had a change of heart and is now more open to hearing what you have to say or what you are offering. Interest and engagement may start to pick up again; you may regain their attention, or they may reconsider what they once said a firm no to. In another interpretation, you may see this card show up when you are in a place where you feel tremendously bored. Nothing seems to spark interest for you; inspiration and creativity are at an all-time low and so is your energy.

## FIVE OF CUPS

"I can only see what I've lost."

Five of Cups is the card of undeniable disappointment. It doesn't matter that there are two cups still standing—it's the three that have been knocked down that have your attention. You can't appreciate what is lingering and left over. This symbolizes those moments in your life where people around you may tell you, "Don't cry over spilled milk." But the reality is that you have experienced some sort of a

loss and you need to mourn it. Depending on the situation you are asking about, it may be helpful to look at what is still left standing and see the good in that. Maybe there is something here that can be salvaged, or maybe for you, the loss of the three is just too great and you need to take time for your suffering.

### Love

The Five of Cups appears when there is an ache or yearning in your heart. Something is missing and feelings of disappointment have rolled in like a dense fog. If you are dating after a breakup, you may be meeting all types of wonderful potential partners, but they are not the person you have been separated from. When this card appears, it is reminding you that it is important to acknowledge this loss, no matter how far in the past; the sting of it still remains. Remember that there are still two cups left, representing the potential for the growth of new feelings. All is not lost, and the Five of Cups can bring partnership and union once again.

### Career/Work

The Five of Cups can point to feelings of unfulfillment and disappointment that have risen inside of you in relation to your work or career. Something about your work life is draining, disappointing, or exhausting. You may have invested your energy or hope into a venture or project only to watch it get knocked over or thrown out. Just like in a general reading, there is a sense of loss. Sometimes that loss is money, effort, security, or safety, or even you or someone close to you losing a job. When the Five of Cups appears, this is Spirit acknowledging that you have experienced some kind of loss and giving you permission to mourn.

### Personal/Spiritual

The Five of Cups shows up as permission to evaluate what you have lost, take time for mourning, and to begin to gather the bits and pieces you need to feel whole again. Cups usually represent our emotions, and here you are experiencing an emotional loss, or you are feeling empty or incomplete.

### Reversed

When reversed, the Five of Cups could bring back what was once taken from you. Somehow those three cups that were knocked over are now upright and filled once again. This is that moment when something you thought was over turns out not to be or someone who has walked out of your life now returns. In readings that show more challenges than opportunities, the Five of Cups reversed symbolizes a person who

can't find light after a loss. They can't seem to stop crying over what has happened. They simply refuse to move on; the emptiness in their heart is just too heavy a weight for them to carry. This card reversed can be a tough one to sit with when it appears in a reading.

## SIX OF CUPS

"Hi, little one! I've missed you. How are you?"

The Six of Cups is easily one of the sweetest cards within the deck! Its common symbolism is two small children—one larger than the other—coming together, with the older one tending to the younger. That's pretty much the vibe of this card—checking in on, tending to, and reconnecting with someone or something you care or cared about. For this reason, the Six of Cups is connected to memories, nostalgia, and feelings of home or family (if this is a comfort, which it very clearly isn't for many people). This card shows up when there is a homecoming on the horizon or you get a text from your ex during Mercury retrograde.

## Love

The amount of times I have seen the Six of Cups show up when people were about to connect with their twin flames or soul mates is absolutely unbelievable. It makes sense because the energy of this card is so sweet and tender, and usually the connection between these two people goes back beyond just this life to the lifetimes before (if you believe in that sort of thing). Either way, it's a feeling of familiarity, of coming "home." It honestly doesn't get much sweeter than that! On the flip side, this can bring back people or events you may rather not run into but that have a way of resurfacing. For example, a toxic ex who texts or calls you at 2 a.m. when you've made it pretty clear that you guys were definitely over. The Six of Cups can suggest feelings of tenderness, but more than anything, it's a card of reconnection.

## Career/Work

The Six of Cups in work-related readings brings back things of the past. This can be an old coworker you run into while getting coffee, a past job offer, or a chance to revisit a lesson or place that will serve your career growth. Because of the maturity gap usually found in this card, you'll see one person (usually a boss or a more knowledgeable person) extending a hand and helping out someone with less experience or influence.

If you recently left one position and moved on to another, this card shows up when you are missing some aspect of the old position even though you are happy and grateful for where you are now.

## Personal/Spiritual

The appearance of the Six of Cups brings a chance for you to understand how your childhood, family, or home upbringing has shaped who you are now. In other readings, this card doesn't dive as deep as childhood but definitely calls in the things and people you wish you could reconnect with. Cups symbolize intuition, so if you are feeling called to reach out to someone you haven't heard from in a while, this card is that nudge to check in and start a conversation. If you are being intuitively guided, it's usually happening for a reason.

## Reversed

When reversed, the Six of Cups brings back memories, but those memories feel like nightmares! These are those lingering thoughts and feelings you wish you could forget or let go of but that keep on resurfacing. I've seen this card show up reversed for those who are stuck in a time that has long since passed—for example, those who were living their best lives in high school or college and now, in adulthood, keep referencing those times. They are stuck in those golden moments, but those old stories feel worn out to those who are forced to keep hearing them. The Six of Cups reversed wants to push people forward, saying, "C'mon! Move on!"

## SEVEN OF CUPS

*"I can't decide! Can I have them all?!"*

The Seven of Cups card can symbolize indecision, being faced with a lot of choices, or feeling (because this is a Cups card, I have to mention feelings!) mentally foggy. You are being presented with too many options—each one different from the one before, and each with their own positives and negatives. How do you choose?! Maybe it's not that you are being presented with a million different options, but that you have so many thoughts and ideas racing in your head that it's almost impossible to focus on just one. Your mind is a storm of activity, and it feels impossible to focus or to have clarity.

### Love
In love readings, the distraction you are feeling may be at an all-time high, as indicated by the Seven of Cups. We see this a lot when people are exploring their options or being told to choose between two people: "It's either *me* or *them*. But you can't have both!" You can see what each person has to offer, but is it possible to choose just one? Maybe you are not sure right now what you want, or maybe life has had you so busy that romance is a bit tough to focus on. Lastly, I've seen this card show up for those who can't see things for what they actually are. Maybe they are being tricked or lied to, maybe they have their head in the clouds, or maybe they want to believe an illusion so much that they are ignoring reality.

### Career/Work
The Seven of Cups can show up for those who are mentally bombarded, overwhelmed, or overworked. There might be a pretty good chance that you're multitasking, but at what cost to your actual productivity? Aside from that, you may find yourself presented with a few different offers, projects, or ideas, and trying to figure out which one will serve you best or which you should start first. You may also find yourself in a "think cloud" (as I like to call it), where

you are brainstorming, working with your imagination, or flipping over ideas.

### Personal/Spiritual
The Seven of Cups here shows up most often when people are mentally foggy, distracted, or disillusioned. Sometimes it can represent the act of escaping reality simply because you are overwhelmed by it. It also may seem as if life is bombarding you with different options or perspectives in a way that may cloud the clarity of your mind or feelings. For the creative types, this card could simply represent the ways you are using your imagination for your own benefit.

### Reversed
The confusion and cloudiness of mind or heart thickens when the Seven of Cups shows up reversed. This is that moment when having a bunch of options feels more paralyzing than liberating, and you are overwhelmed by the options. Maybe you can't make up your mind at all or maybe your inability to focus or choose has you missing out on all of the opportunities, not just one. Alternately, it's possible that this card will show up when you have finally decided on what you want or should do next or when clarity starts to resurface again for you.

# EIGHT OF CUPS

"What is in front of me isn't enough. I need to pack up and go."

Eight of Cups brings disappointment, sadness, and a realization that what has been offered to you or given to you is not at all what you want or deserve. The eight cups have been reviewed and stacked, meaning that you know everything you need to know, you've seen all you need to see, and still it is not enough. This card shows up when it is time for you to move forward and say goodbye. It almost always brings heavy feelings of sadness because, maybe if you had your way, things would have worked out differently and you could stay. As hard as the message of this card is to receive, remember that after the sadness of the Eight of Cups, the rewards of the Nine of Cups follow quickly after. Anytime you say goodbye to one thing, you are also saying hello to something else. If the universe and life are guiding you forward, it is always for your highest and greatest good.

## Love

When the Eight of Cups shows up, it is time for you to say goodbye in a relationship or move forward with your life, no matter how difficult it may seem. Someone is either thinking about leaving or has already begun the process of moving forward and on. The feelings behind the Eight of Cups are typically pretty heavy, especially when there is a history between you and another person. This card can show that someone is needing to move away (maybe for work). They'd rather not leave, and it's with a heavy heart that they are walking forward. Maybe you have to say goodbye to someone after a wonderful weekend or month together, as we often see in long-distance relationships. In lighter readings, the Eight of Cups is someone who is begrudgingly trying something new to find love.

## Career/Work

You are moving forward from a work situation that is not making you happy or fulfilled, as indicated by the Eight of Cups. Maybe your job has asked you to travel to a new location or maybe you have happily quit but are sad to say goodbye to the coworkers you've grown to love. Either way, there is a "goodbye" of sorts happening here and the nudge to move forward into the future. Because the Eight of Cups signals

disappointment or sadness, you may be forced to leave your work environment and are not sure what the future holds. Just like in a general reading, this card reminds you that when you have to end one thing, you are also opening the door to a new chapter. Stack your cups carefully and respectfully and move forward into the next phase of your journey!

## Personal/Spiritual

The Eight of Cups is usually a tough pill to swallow because so much sadness is connected with it. For whatever reason, your current situation is not making you happy or serving you; you are being guided to let it go and release yourself to start over fresh someplace new. For some, this could be an actual change in your location, while for others it could mean putting to rest old habits that have blocked your growth or no longer serve your overall well-being. Saying goodbye can be hard, and this card acknowledges that.

## Reversed

There are two meanings for the Eight of Cups when it is reversed. The first is that someone you had to say goodbye to in the past is reentering your life. The cups that were neatly stacked when upright have brought that person back because they desire what they have left behind. The second meaning is that someone is refusing to move forward despite knowing that the situation they are in is not likely to work out or is destructive to their well-being and happiness. The Eight of Cups has shown you all that you need to see, but you'd rather stay in the muck or stickiness of the situation versus risk saying goodbye and seeing what else might be out there. For you, it seems that something may still be salvageable in the situation you have now.

## NINE OF CUPS

**"My wish has been granted!"**

In the tarot world, we all understand the Nine of Cups to represent a wish that has come true. Although that may be what has happened for you, the Nine of Cups more than anything illustrates the feeling of contentment, of being totally satisfied, proud, and even a little smug with yourself. The number 9 brings an energy of completion, and in this moment, you are happy with how far you've come and what you have been rewarded with. This is why it is the card of wish fulfillment—because you are feeling happy with what has finally manifested!

### Love
What you've been waiting and hoping for is soon to manifest . . . if it hasn't already! The Nine of Cups brings pleasure, joy, contentment, and satisfaction to your reading and relationship. If you are waiting for someone special, they may just show up and check all the boxes you were hoping for in a partner. If you are partnered, the relationship is taking a turn where things just seem to be "right." Maybe you couldn't be happier! Not to be negative, but I have to cover all my bases, and I have often seen this card show up for those who have become a little "too comfortable" in their relationship and feel like they don't need to put any more work in. This is something to look out for in otherwise troubling relationship readings.

### Career/Work
When the Nine of Cups appears in work-related readings, it really seems as if you couldn't be happier with your career at the moment! This card relates to that feeling you get the day after you've been promoted—the surprise has worn off, but the happy feeling lingers on and you're grateful for the

good news and proud of your progress! More often than not, the Nine of Cups brings good feelings with it, but occasionally, it can point toward a person who seems smug, overly confident, or cocky in the work environment, someone you are most likely already aware of.

## Personal/Spiritual

The Nine of Cups brings a feeling of getting exactly what you wanted or wished for. Nine is the number of completion: The lessons you've learned and even the heartaches you've experienced have brought you to this very moment, and you're so proud that you want to say out loud, "Look, I've finally made it!" We can view this card as expressing confidence or smugness, but for most people, this is only because the journey to get to this point has been so tough and the road so long. The nine cups collected symbolize major moments and experiences in your life that have led you to this point. In personal readings, it shows you that there is a need to do what is right for you and what will make you most happy. This card is not focused on others but on your own joy and well-being. This is that moment in your life when you realize that self-care is a must and not at all selfish.

## Reversed

Nine of Cups reversed still has the potential to bring a feeling of satisfaction or a sense that your wish has manifested, but it's either delayed or comes at a price. This is a moment when you question, "Am I ever going to see this wish manifest itself in my life?" Or it may express the feeling you have when you receive what you've been wanting for so long, but it still doesn't seem right or make you happy. Maybe it's not what you were expecting or maybe what you had to go through to get it—the struggles and the sacrifices or even the delay—makes it feel like it wasn't worth it. You could also have been neglecting your own self-care and happiness in your attempts to reach your goal to the point where your emotional balance is off, and you can't really enjoy the fruits of your labor because you're emotionally exhausted or drained.

# TEN OF CUPS

## "My dream is finally coming true!"

The heart is filled when the Ten of Cups makes an appearance in your reading. This is because each of the ten cups on the card represents a positive memory, event, or simply something to be grateful for. This card reminds you to count your blessings and acknowledge how far you've come. But more than that, it brings total happiness because you have received (or are soon going to receive) everything you've ever wanted! The Ten of Cups represents time spent with family, entering a space of deep true love, or the bliss you feel when you lose yourself in your work while doing what you love. Feelings of emotional fullness surge and your "cup of life" is filled!

## Love

You may be feeling like you have found your soul mate, are celebrating true love, or even marriage when the Ten of Cups makes an appearance! This card is associated with family and lasting bonds, so it appears a lot when you are preparing to build your own forever with someone special. Your heart is so filled that it feels like you've really found your own "happily ever after." Whatever dream or experience you are seeking when you asked the cards your question has the potential to give you great joy and pleasure.

## Career/Work

You've really found your soul's calling when the Ten of Cups appears for you in a career reading! The feeling of wholeness that comes with this card is undeniable. You are not only enjoying your work but also have a sense that what you are doing serves a greater purpose. This card can also suggest that you spend time with coworkers at events designed to allow you to have fun while getting to know each other better—for example, at a work-related party or barbecue. If you have not achieved a deeper sense of purpose in your work life, this card encourages you to keep your hope and faith alive. It tells you not to give up on finding the kind of work that will truly make you happy!

## Personal/Spiritual

The Ten of Cups is concerned with your feelings of fulfillment and the sense that you have found your source of happiness here on earth, at least for the moment. This card is what nirvana feels like after meditation—you are one with the world and nothing can ruffle your feathers! What is it that brings you bliss? What will complete the picture for you? That is what this card represents for you now, as well as the chance to enjoy the present moment for all that it is. Lastly, you could find yourself spending time with people you love or maybe even happily alone doing exactly what your heart desires!

## Reversed

When the Ten of Cups is reversed, those feelings of joy and bliss you can experience when this card is upright are blocked. This could be that moment when you are at a family gathering, but your favorite family member or the person you love can't be there to enjoy the moment with you. The feelings of fun and pleasure should be there, but instead, it feels like something or someone is missing. It's possible you are doubting that your own dream of "happily ever after" can even happen; will you have to live the rest of your life without the very things you desire the most? You may find yourself really struggling to find a sense of purpose in your work, or it just doesn't give you the same feelings of joy that it once did. It's also possible that your dream has manifested, but something still feels like it's missing.

# PENTACLES

**ASTROLOGICAL
SIGNS:** Taurus, Virgo,
Capricorn

**ELEMENT:** Earth

The Pentacles are ruled by
earth, which connects them
with material wealth, resources,
commitment, money, and
security. You'll see these cards
show up to represent someone's
level of commitment (if any),
what type of investments or
help they are receiving and/or
giving, and what is being built.
The energy of earth is practical
and realistic, so that is mirrored
in the mind-set of the cards.

ACE of PENTACLES.

"The first seed of
commitment and
investment is in my
hands ready to be
planted."

The Ace of Pentacles
represents the beginning
stage of something you
are creating, something that you feel ready
to invest in and build. *Investment* is the
keyword because energy, money, resources,
effort, and most important, commitment, are
all needed here. This card doesn't appear
lightly. It is serious about creating a solid
foundation to support a long-term plan or
vision. The suit of Pentacles naturally connects with money, but more than that, it is
about what you value and are willing to
gladly tend in order to watch this coin
multiply and thrive.

## Love

One word—*commitment*. The Ace of
Pentacles is the card of potential for commitment and promises. When you pull this card,
you or someone else may know what you
want romantically but will usually not take
shortcuts or cheat to get to the finish line.

This promise that you (or they) make has the potential to be lasting. The goal is to build a solid relationship. Because this card only shows you the beginning of the journey, you will need to be patient. You will both need to put in a lot of work and time to make this bond grow. If you're waiting to hear from someone you like or love . . . well, just know you're going to be waiting awhile! This card is so slow—like, so slow. But it promises that you will hear from your beloved—when they are ready and have checked everything else off their list first.

## Career/Work

To see the Ace of Pentacles in a career reading is to know that abundance, returns on investments, or a new job offer are pretty much yours. If you are waiting to hear back about a job—it's yours. If you are busting your tail for a promotion—that, too, is most likely yours. If you are starting a business, putting down roots, and investing a little money now, this card says that risk will pay off. The Ace of Pentacles points to signing checks, agreeing to deals, getting paid, and building your resources. It guides you to be slow, realistic, hardworking, patient, and practical. Have a plan, work toward it, and you will see a promising start to your potential growth and reward.

## Personal/Spiritual

Patience is everything with the Ace of Pentacles—patience and practicality. Are you willing to put in the work that will result in real personal progress? Well, let's begin. Start with a realistic plan (emphasis on realistic!), commit to it, and stick with it. That's the message this card brings. Shortcuts don't exist with this card, and if you try to create them or take them, you will regret it. Invest in yourself—physically, mentally, and spiritually. Make the time to give yourself what you need.

## Reversed

Yikes—the Ace of Pentacles reversed suggests that the investment you made or the time you put in seems to be a lost cause. Either you or someone else is pulling out, having a change of heart, and no longer sees the same value as they did before. They don't want to exert the same energy they originally started off with. A contract or agreement could be broken. A commitment is called off or questioned. Are you faithful and committed? Do you want to see this venture grow, or would you rather walk away and abandon it? How much do you have to lose and is it worth it to try to salvage what is left?

# TWO OF PENTACLES

## "I'm juggling to make ends meet."

Multitasking—doing whatever you need to do to get the work done—is what comes to mind with the Two of Pentacles. It seems like you're not really able to move forward right now (if you even really wanted to) because you are stuck in this current limbo phase of juggling everything that's currently on your plate. This works for a little bit because there is value in doing all you can to help your projects achieve liftoff. But, at some point, you are going to need to ask for help; you'll need another hand. The Two of Pentacles is the card of doing more than one thing at one time to keep balance and momentum.

## Love

The Two of Pentacles can be pretty tricky in love relationships. Whether you're single or paired up, it seems like you have too much on your plate right now trying to balance your work and personal life and perhaps wanting to please your partner. If you weren't so committed to your goals, I'm not sure you would juggle all this for as long as you have. But because you are invested, you do whatever you can to keep the ball rolling. You may easily feel in over your head—or at least challenged—by your many responsibilities and expectations. This card may also symbolize having multiple partners, many dating options, or exploring your options before choosing the one you think is worth investing in.

## Career/Work

Activity picks up in the work world for you . . . or at least your many tasks and obligations are building, as indicated by the Two of Pentacles. It's that feeling of e-mails pouring in, orders needing to be filled, meetings needing to be held, and your phone blowing up with calls. Maybe for a few days it's okay and you can chalk it up to a busy week, but if it goes on longer than that, it can become truly exhausting. Are you building a business from the ground up and swamped with doing all you can to get it underway? Is extra work somehow being magically funneled over to your desk? Are you overwhelmed with a packed schedule? All of these are common when the Two of Pentacles pops up.

## Personal/Spiritual

When the Two of Pentacles appears, this may be a good time to review how much you have agreed to carry on your plate. This card understands that you are capable of multitasking and juggling all of your many responsibilities, but should you? And, if so, for how long? Consider these questions wisely. For the time being, you may be doing all you can to juggle your obligations with the hope that it will pay off and carry you to the finish line.

## Reversed

When reversed, all the balls that the Two of Pentacles has been working so hard to keep up in the air start to fall to the ground. You simply cannot carry on doing everything you've been doing. You are overworked, overwhelmed, and stressed out. Because Pentacles so often deals with commitment, it's possible that someone or something that was originally there to help you has now bailed. Or maybe your plan wasn't developed strongly enough to carry the weight of the responsibility for too long. Either way, you may be losing the balance; you can't hold it all together.

## THREE OF PENTACLES

"I value your work—can I commission you to make something for me?"

The Three of Pentacles brings recognition—people acknowledging how hard you've been working and how talented you are and deciding they want to invest in you. Think of this as the gifted musician who plays their violin in the city streets, starts to draw a crowd, gains a reputation for their talent, signs a record deal, and is suddenly the next rock-star violinist! This is what you are experiencing with the Three of Pentacles in a reading—a metaphorical (or maybe literal) crowd is growing around you, people are noticing your gift, and they are usually finding ways to show that they are ready to build alongside you.

## Love

With the Three of Pentacles, your partner (or potential partner) sees something special and unique in you. For this reason, you may find yourself in the developing stages of building solidity in your relationship or working together to resolve issues. Usually both parties are bringing equal effort into the relationship because they see the value in committing the time and effort. In readings where you are single, it's possible that you are focused on your work life to the point where your love life may take a back seat for the moment. You may also have found someone you really like but are looking to see where this relationship might be headed. Perhaps you are about to have the "What exactly are we?" conversation.

### Career/Work
I can't promise you that investors or promotions will come pouring in when the Three of Pentacles appears, but people are definitely beginning to take note of your work! This card tends to draw a little bit of a crowd; people are watching what you are creating with an eye toward potentially investing in you to see you create more. This card also suggests teamwork to make the dream work! Your coworkers or alliances are joining forces to bring your unique skill sets together to create something amazing. If you work on commission, this is the moment when a client chooses you.

### Personal/Spiritual
The Three of Pentacles brings the energy of hard work, investment in talent or resources, and connection with others with like-minded goals. More often than not, you are working with people or meeting with groups for your own growth. If you are working alone, this card suggests you pay attention to the details of your progress toward your own personal goals. The Three of Pentacles can represent self-improvement activities (such as yoga or guided meditation) or even travel that you may undertake to expand your knowledge.

### Reversed
Reversed, the Three of Pentacles brings problems. This is when people have invested in a project but are getting work that is not what was promised or that is sloppily thrown together. For whatever reason, the work that was put in is disappointing and may need to be redone with a higher level of quality and concentration. Maybe there is an investor who decides last minute to break a contract, so the work that was put in gets lost or comes to a standstill. If you are working with a group, not everyone is putting in their fair share and someone will inevitably end up carrying the weight of the workload. You or someone in your life may find yourselves taking a big step backward when the Three of Pentacles emerges reversed.

# FOUR OF PENTACLES

*"I worked so hard for what I have. I'm never letting go!"*

Think of an artist who is commissioned to create an incredible masterpiece and puts their heart and soul into the project. When it's time to give the finished piece to the client, the artist's experience is bittersweet because of the amount of effort they have put into its creation. Well, that is what we are seeing with the Four of Pentacles. You have or someone around you has worked so hard to build something, and you need to take a moment alone to enjoy the tangible fruit of all that effort. This card can be stubborn, unmoving, and even a little selfish, but only because the person in question has invested so much in this project. The Four of Pentacles is about holding on to what you have and not wanting to let go, enjoying your sense of stability, and maybe even saving for a rainy day.

## Love
There are two sides to the Four of Pentacles in love relationships. The first one is that you are so happy with the progress of your relationship that you don't want to disrupt the status quo. Think of new couples who are deeply in love. All they want to do is spend time with each other and lock themselves away from the rest of the world. Good luck getting them to hang out separately with their old friends like they did when they were single! This stubbornness and unwillingness to move or budge is very Four of Pentacles. The other side of this card points to a state of mind that is not open to new energy (such as meeting new people, going out and dating, or even leaving the house) or that is emotionally closed off. This isn't always a bad thing—sometimes people just need time to themselves for healing or are simply not open to compromise.

## Career/Work
Pentacles is 100 percent connected to finances, money, and investing, so if the Four of Pentacles appears, you may be saving for a rainy day or working hard to create security for yourself. You could find yourself dealing with a client or coworker who is stubborn or difficult to work with. While they might just be set in their ways, maybe it's you who refuses to budge. This card discourages risk-taking at this time because more than anything it wants you to hold on to what you've worked so hard to build. If you are

waiting for a promotion or growth, this card indicates that this is also not coming at this time. Others may be locked into their positions and are not willing to provide more finances than they have already given. Negotiations tend to hit a standstill as people are not likely to budge, bend, or compromise.

### Personal/Spiritual

In spiritual readings, the Four of Pentacles symbolizes the universe giving you permission to be more selfish with your time and energy. Maybe you are in need of some healing or time alone before you dive into your next big adventure. People may be trying to pull you out, but it's okay to do what you need to do and not compromise. This card also represents enjoying and holding on to what you have now and feeling grateful for the sense of security that it brings you. You might also be working on saving or budgeting to help build your bank account even further.

### Reversed

When reversed, the Four of Pentacles turns from representing a healthy stubbornness to flat-out stinginess. This card refuses to share with others, is hoarding resources, and is definitely not interested in investing. This becomes a problem because we need flexibility in order to grow. For example,

sometimes you need to take a healthy risk, spending money to gain money. People are shut down and shutting you out—or maybe you're the one who is remaining stiff and untrusting of others.

## FIVE OF PENTACLES

"Left in the cold to fend for yourself."

The Five of Pentacles signifies loss, but more than that, there is a feeling of abandonment or you are in need. Their sense of security is ripped out from under the person involved with this question, they've fallen on some pretty hard times, and they are in need of a helping hand to pull them back to their feet. This card brings financial change that is not only unpredictable but creates a shock that most people don't want to experience. Homelessness, poverty, sickness, and suffering come with the coldness of this card.

### Love

In love readings, the feeling of being abandoned is very, very strong with the Five of

Pentacles. You are feeling alone, isolated, or forgotten, or your overall sense of self-esteem or self-worth seems to have plummeted. This card shows up often for people whose hearts have gone through a lot or are now taking a beating. They are wondering if there are good people out there, if they will ever really find love, or if they will have to settle for a "less than" relationship or crumbs of affection. Just as in the general reading, you may find yourself needing to ask for help (for example, counseling) to process the loss you have experienced.

### Career/Work
The Five of Pentacles is a tough card to receive in career-related readings. For some reason, you've been kicked out into the cold. Maybe you've been fired from your job, you're struggling to find opportunities, or you're not making enough to pay the bills. If a client is supposed to be paying you, there is a chance you may not receive it. If you are waiting to hear if you got the job, the odds aren't in your favor. Check and recheck your budgets and finances to make room and space for a rainy day.

### Personal/Spiritual
I've seen the Five of Pentacles come up for a lot for people who are questioning their faith in a higher power, their purpose, or even their value. Life's challenges have applied so much pressure that you may feel like you are going to break. You're not sure whether you will find the answers you are seeking or the help you need, and you don't know if you will ever bounce back strong again. In personal readings, you may really be feeling left out, alone, or isolated from a group. This is that beautiful person in a room full of people who still never feels like they fit in. Parts of you are looking for your home, your sense of belonging, your tribe.

### Reversed
Five of Pentacles reversed drags this feeling of isolation and hopelessness out longer than anybody deserves to experience it. This card may arise reversed when you have tried to connect with others, you've asked for help, and you've reached out to all your resources, but it still seems like nothing is coming together for you. Maybe there is a drought of resources or potential in your area. I have also seen this card show up for people who are in state of impoverishment but refuse to ask for or accept help, so they never give themselves a chance to climb up out of their current condition.

# SIX OF PENTACLES

*"Can you make a donation or give to help my cause?"*

The Six of Pentacles is the card of give-and-take. This card represents receiving a helping hand from another. Or maybe you are the one offering advice or resources to someone less fortunate than you. That's a wonderful thing, but the problem comes when we look into *why* the offering is made. You see, the balance of this card is off a bit. Someone is perhaps being generous with you and with the amount they are agreeing to share—but you can't reciprocate. Or the giver has more than the receiver, and the receiver is still in lack. In love relationships, this can be problematic (I'll talk about that in a moment). Otherwise, you are getting a little extra from the universe than you would normally have received.

## Love
With the Six of Pentacles, there is give-and-take happening in your love relationship, but the balance is not equal. Sure, you may be receiving attention, affection, or love, but

this card indicates that whatever was given may not be enough. While dating, you may be giving just enough to say you've tried but may not be fully investing. The chemistry and spark simply may not be there, or it's possible that you are spending your attention and energy elsewhere.

## Career/Work
The Six of Pentacles fares better in a career reading than it does in a love reading, so you can breathe a sigh of relief with its appearance here. For the most part, this card suggests a little extra cash money coming your way. It may come in the form of an investor, some guidance, or even some labor to help take the load off your shoulders for a bit. If these are not voluntarily given to you, you may be the one who needs to ask for them. At the same time, it is equally possible that the roles are reversed, and you are the one called to help or invest in others.

## Personal/Spiritual
There is a need to lend assistance or ask for a helping hand when the Six of Pentacles appears. Don't be afraid to ask for more, especially if it will make your life easier. Even though the Pentacles usually represent tangible things like money or offerings, in readings focused around spirituality, I have seen this card show up for people who were

relying on the help and guidance of their angels, guides, or a higher power to provide more insight into their lives. On the flip side, you may be called to help others less fortunate than you. We all have ways that we can help each other out, even if you feel you have nothing to give. This is a chance for sharing and generosity.

## Reversed

Yikes and double yikes—reversed, the Six of Pentacles shows that you or someone around you is in need, but there is literally no one around to help them; there's nobody to pull them to their feet. If you were to receive some kind of help now, it comes with a price, the assistance somehow adding to the weight of your current debt. If you are trying to pay off loans or bills, it seems that they are building up faster than you can pay them, and there is little to no real help around to bail you out. When this card shows up in love readings, this is that moment when there is a little bit of blackmail and a partner may say, "I gave you what you wanted. What more do you want from me?!" when in reality their effort was half-hearted at best.

# SEVEN OF PENTACLES

"Will my efforts ever pay off?"

You're at that phase in your journey where you are wondering if you see things working out. Pentacles is all about effort, commitment, and financial reward, but right now, your patience and your commitment are being seriously tested. If you put in more work, will you see the reward? Or will it all have been for nothing? This card suggests taking a step back and examining what you are asking about to decide if additional work and effort are really worth it. Looking at things from a different perspective will help you see the bigger picture and figure out what needs to be tweaked to create success.

## Love

In love, when the Seven of Pentacles appears, you are wondering how to make things work and if they even will work. You have put a lot of effort into creating a stable or healthy relationship, but for some reason, love and effort may not be enough. If both people are willing to work together, this card represents the potential they are putting into building a stronger bond and learning from past mistakes. If single, you are examining yourself and your needs in a relationship closely. What kind of relationship do you want? What areas of yourself are willing to compromise? What aspects of you need healing? What are you ready for?

### Career/Work

The Seven of Pentacles asks you to take a step back to look at the bigger picture of your work environment or a project you've been building. Maybe you're examining several different offers that have been placed in front of you, trying to decide which one is the best for you. This card can suggest comparison, but more than this, it is a healthy examination of what you are willing to adjust to and commit to. If you don't see growth or potential in a project, there is a high chance you should reevaluate your commitment and maybe even back out. If you decide it will be worth it, you will dedicate yourself to a great amount of work and the effort. But you won't regret it!

### Personal/Spiritual

We have a limited time here on earth, and no one wants to waste it, including you. With the Seven of Pentacles, you are being called by the universe to examine your path and

progress in life. Are you happy with where you are? What do you need to adjust to feel whole, happy, and complete? This is an important moment in your journey. With this card, you will know clearly what steps you need to take, what you are ready for and preparing for, and what intentions you need to set for the future.

### Reversed

Reversed, the Seven of Pentacles feels like you will not see the payoff you were expecting despite the amount of time and energy you put into your goal. For some reason, you suspect that, even if you put more work in, it will not make a difference. It seems better to walk away, because adding more effort or energy will just end up exhausting you or making the situation worse. In some readings, this card reversed is showing you that you may have ignored the call to step back and see what areas you needed to adjust so that your time and energy could be used constructively and efficiently. Not all progress is good progress; pausing to take stock of the situation would have helped you tremendously in knowing where to place your effort next.

# EIGHT OF PENTACLES

*"I'm going to show them what I'm made of!"*

The Eight of Pentacles is the card of hard work, dedication, and commitment. This is the moment in your life when you are paying attention to detail and are working toward your goal, canceling out all distraction to create high-quality work. Someone has invested in you, and you are now working to meet that expectation. This card never takes shortcuts; in fact, it tends to go above and beyond to exceed expectations. If others didn't find your talents worthy of investing in, trust me, they wouldn't. When this card appears, it means that it's time for you to show your supporters or collaborators what you're made of!

## Love

In love relationships, the Eight of Pentacles confirms that you are doing all you can to invest your energy into building a healthy, loving, and lasting relationship. You know exactly what you want, and your efforts are showing results. Nine times out of ten, your determination will pay off, because with the energy of the Eight of Pentacles, people really see the amount of effort and dedication you're putting in. If you are single, this symbolizes that you are ready to commit and apply yourself to the right partnership.

## Career/Work

When the Eight of Pentacles appears in a career-related reading, it reveals how invested you are in the quality of your work. You are ready to do whatever it takes to build something substantial. You may be paying close attention to detail to make sure that the work you do—whether for a boss or for a client—is excellent, and nothing less. Because the Pentacles suit is connected to money and finances, you may also be finding yourself managing budgets or employees. Either way, your head is down, you're focused, and you're doing whatever it takes to get the job done well.

## Personal/Spiritual

In spiritual readings, the Eight of Pentacles declares that you want a fulfilling and meaningful life. You don't want to take shortcuts toward your happiness. In fact, you are not afraid to examine the sides of yourself you're not proud of in order to heal them and turn that weakness into strength. Because you are so invested in your own growth, you will, without a doubt, see the reward. The Eight of Pentacles acknowledges you for the effort you've put in even if no one else sees it. If you're proud of yourself at the end of the day, then that's what matters the most!

## Reversed

When reversed, the Eight of Pentacles indicates that someone may be taking shortcuts or submitting less than high-quality work. Maybe they decided halfway through the project that they weren't going to commit themselves to doing whatever it took to create something of quality. Maybe the resources needed to do a job well fizzled out or your passion or motivation died. And, in other readings, if you have applied yourself and done a job well, people may not acknowledge or appreciate it. When the Eight of Pentacles is reversed, there is impatience, you can't concentrate, and people are cheating or scamming you. You may even lose your job.

# NINE OF PENTACLES

"Look at all that I have manifested and created!"

You're in a phase in your life right now where you can enjoy the fruits of your labor. In most tarot decks, the Nine of Pentacles shows a woman walking through a garden, feeling like a queen. She's looking at all that she has worked to accomplish; she feels grateful, safe, and secure, and so well taken care of. Considering the long journey that got her to this point, she deserves it! The Nine of Pentacles is showing you what you are working toward or have currently achieved. Others may look from the outside and tell you how lucky you are, but the reality is that it took a lot of sweat and effort to reach this point. It's not just luck. With this card, security and financial abundance are yours. You can take care of yourself. You're standing alone in a lot of ways—perhaps self-employed or independent—and, with this card, you can see the reality of what you have achieved.

## Love

When the Nine of Pentacles appears, you are feeling separate from a partner. Maybe you are single and though you would like a partner, it isn't something you feel you must have to experience happiness and wholeness. You are feeling totally empowered and independent because you know that you are all you need. If you are in a relationship, there is a sense of independence: You and your partner may happily live separate lives. You do your thing and your partner does theirs, and it works for you. There is one more thing I need to mention with this card: Although wealth and security are very important, they are not everything. This card acknowledges that you are independent, but it also wants you to be open to receiving more when it comes to love, intimacy, and affection. The Nine of Pentacles reminds you that you deserve that romantic reward as well.

## Career/Work

The Nine of Pentacles brings the energy of independence and self-sufficiency. Often in career readings, this card is pointing to a person who is self-employed. Whether or not this is the case, the card represents material security and an overall sense of well-being and success. Yes, you can accomplish and achieve even more, but the reality is that you don't have to. You're in a good place in your life right now where your needs are being met, you have sufficient finances, and there's wiggle room for spending. Whatever has been working for you is something you want to continue, even if maybe a little later on you can decide to adjust it accordingly. But right now, you're enjoying the fruits of your labor!

## Personal/Spiritual

In personal readings, the Nine of Pentacles give you permission to take the alone time you need to achieve peace and a sense of well-being. This card does not at all focus on what others are doing. It wants you to do what's in your best interest and to enjoy your time indulgently. You may find yourself going on a solo trip, taking a retreat, or spending time in nature. The Pentacles are ruled by the element of earth so nature is where you will most likely find yourself being restored. Your main focus is on maintaining material security, but also on gratitude, enjoying the moment, and using your time in the way that serves you best.

## Reversed

When reversed, the Nine of Pentacles represents the moment when you realize that money can't buy your happiness. You might have all the resources and wealth in the world, but it doesn't fill the void in your heart.

With this card reversed, it feels like your success and your achievement mean nothing. Maybe everything you have worked for or been given seems to have been ripped out from under you, leaving you with no sense of safety or security. You may be feeling vulnerable and threatened. Your self-esteem may be low, and you may find yourself relying on others to provide for you instead of being able to provide for yourself.

## TEN OF PENTACLES

"My family is my wealth."

The Ten of Pentacles dives deeply into wealth. You have not only achieved financial stability but also a level of success that can provide for you in this life—and maybe even support generations to come. When the Ten of Pentacles appears, you may be on the receiving end of huge levels of profit from past investments. They are paying off now, and you are seriously reaping the reward! There's a strong tie to ancestors and family, and a bond to a provider with deeply rooted resources. You're feeling safe, comfortable, and stable. You're definitely not worried about where your next meal is coming from—in fact, you are more likely to be planning some wonderful vacation! The Ten of Pentacles is known to be the trust fund baby of the tarot deck.

### Love
When the Ten of Pentacles appears in a love reading, I always wonder if there are family expectations for a relationship or even if there's an arranged marriage type of situation. This is because the ties to family are very strong with the Ten of Pentacles; it signifies that a mind-set you carry into your current relationship may bring a generational perspective. You may find that you are doing what your family has done before you—for good or for bad. Sometimes with this card, you find yourself choosing partners based on how they can provide for you or how you can provide for them. You not only want commitment and stability for yourself, but you are also thinking about wealth. In an existing relationship, your commitment to the partnership is almost unbreakable. The Ten of Pentacles is very established, and it signifies a set routine—so to step away from a partnership almost seems impossible because one or both partners are heavily devoted to this bond.

## Career/Work

The Ten of Pentacles shows that moment when you are focused on achieving incredible success in your work life. You want wealth and security that is not only lasting but abundantly serves you so that you can help not only yourself but also your extended family. When this card appears, the business deals you are making are almost set in stone and will most likely serve you generously in the years to come. You are feeling wise with your money, you are informed in your decision-making, and you will receive the benefit of careful thinking and planning.

## Personal/Spiritual

When the Ten of Pentacles shows up, you may find yourself diving into the wounds of your ancestors and exploring the ways your family ties and behavioral patterns have worked to shape you. The things you want most for yourself are stability, safety, and security, but you're also realizing that emotional well-being and peace of mind are equally important. The decisions you're making for your well-being are not just in service of the temporary moment; they will affect your reality for years to come. You want to make sure these decisions will serve you in healthy, constructive ways for the rest of your life. Having a firm foundation where you feel stable will support your growth at this time.

## Reversed

With a reversed Ten of Pentacles, it seems as though all you know could be crumbling around you. What you thought would be lasting and permanent may evaporate overnight, leaving you feeling unsure and unsafe. This is when the security you thought was solid seems to disappear, and time seems to be running out to figure out what the heck to do next! There is definitely a sense of loss: The wealth you may have accumulated somehow feels isolating and cold, or there are fights between your family members over money. Maybe an inheritance doesn't seem fair or people are in disagreement about how the money is allotted. The plans you originally made now need to be switched up tremendously, but the vibe around your situation or question may be really stubborn at the moment; the struggle to move forward is intense.

# SWORDS

**ASTROLOGICAL SIGNS:**
Aquarius, Gemini, Libra

**ELEMENT:** Air

The Swords deal with the power of the mind, intellect, and words, all of which are ruled by the element of air. You'll see how words and thoughts can change or destroy things, for good or for evil. These cards want to communicate, learn, and understand because they have a natural curious energy; they are also emotionally detached, which can create tension in intimate relationships. Sword cards show up with cool colors—silver, black, and white—because that is how they operate: coolly and directly.

# ACE OF SWORDS

*"I deliver the cold hard slap of truth."*

The Ace of Swords represents the power of the mind and your word as well as the strength of your will. When this card shows up in a spread, it is a reminder of how you can use those three things to shape or destroy your own destiny. Easily, this sword is double-edged. You can use it to help and protect yourself or others, or it can be turned on you and become a tool of destruction. For this reason, you need to be very careful and aware of the decisions you make and how the consequences of your actions will unfold. The Ace of Swords is the card of tremendous intellectual strengths. It cuts out all emotion so that you can make the most logical decision, even if it is difficult or painful. With this card, you want to cut through all of the bull. You're making the obstacles that would have stopped you work for you by being disciplined, thinking before you act, knowing exactly what you want, and articulating it clearly.

## Love

In love relationships, the Ace of Swords struggles because it does not tap into feelings, intuition, or emotions. It is rational and logical, and that is how it approaches the idea of love. To the Ace of Swords, if something doesn't make sense, it won't work, and if it doesn't have the potential to work, the Ace of Swords energy doesn't see the purpose of it—at least for now. This is a time for you to be clear about your intentions and your will. You can talk with your partner about your relationship expectations, but what comes up may be a little hard to swallow comfortably—what you hear may not be what you want to hear. At least now you know.

## Career/Work

In career readings, the Ace of Swords gives you the power to assert yourself clearly and precisely. You are using the power of rational and logical thinking to achieve and accomplish your goals. This is where you'll find the most success in your work life. Your mind is focused and sharp, and your ability to concentrate is like a razor blade cutting through Jell-O. Nothing can stand in your way. Because the source of this card's energy is Justice from the Major Arcana, you may find yourself drawn to careers connected with law and order, maintaining balance, and doing the things that most people don't have the heart or the capacity to do.

## Personal/Spiritual

Here the Ace of Swords again reminds you of your own tremendous power. You are clearly defining what you do and don't want for yourself, and you are creating boundaries to protect what you know is rightfully yours. The Ace of Swords is calling in the energies of the universe to manifest your desires because the power of your word and your mind is clear and focused. Know exactly what you want because that is what's coming.

## Reversed

When reversed, the Ace of Swords is incredibly destructive. This is when the words we say and the thoughts we think are hurtful and maybe even abusive. Perhaps someone is not thinking before they speak, or perhaps they are hurting people because they themselves are also hurting and they'll say whatever they can to make others suffer. This is when we see words used for evil such as gossip or written slander. It is heartless and cold, and people suffer as a result. You need to be careful that you are not your own worst enemy at this time because again, the blade of this sword has two edges and what you put out there is exactly what you will eventually receive.

# TWO OF SWORDS

"I don't know what I should do . . . "

The Two of Swords in a reading lets you know that no movement should be made at this time. It's time to pause and reflect. You are in a space where you are probably guarding your heart and need time to step back so that you can reconnect to the truth of what is right and best for you. It seems like you may not know exactly what you want, and that is why you're taking time to ask yourself questions before you actually make any decisions. There's a delay, you are waiting, or you may be feeling overwhelmed and weighing the pros and cons before you make your next move.

## Love

In love, the Two of Swords reflects the idea that no one seems to be making a move or they don't want to share their feelings. A relationship seems to be stuck; you're not really sure how to articulate what it is that you've been thinking or feeling, and so you may need additional time to figure things out. If you are just coming out of a relationship, this card represents a need to allow the dust to settle; you may have just been really hurt and you need time for yourself. Again, your heart is guarded, and you are not willing right now to jump into something else without knowing exactly what you're getting into. Often, I see this card show up when someone is trying to make sense of what is going on around them and within them. Sometimes what helps is to disconnect from your emotions and your hopes for a relationship (if you're in one), and look realistically at the pros and the cons so that you can decide for yourself what the right thing to do next is.

## Career/Work

The Two of Swords indicates that you're not able to make a move right now in regard to your career. It almost seems as if you're stuck in limbo. Maybe you're waiting for a client to decide if they're going to work with you or maybe you've run out of ideas for what you want to do next. Either way, you're stuck in the current status quo and nothing is moving forward. If you're waiting for a job, you're going to be waiting for a while because your potential future boss hasn't made up their mind yet. This card represents indecision—being suspended—and there's not much you can do to get this ball rolling. In fact, sometimes it's best to just wait until things become clear and you can figure out which move makes the most sense logically.

### Personal/Spiritual

I always see the Two of Swords in readings for someone who is in need of some serious healing time, and you really need to give yourself permission to do this. You feel you cannot make any moves or decisions right now, and this is usually because you have been through so much emotionally or you simply don't know what to do next. Sometimes, not knowing is absolutely okay, normal, and natural. If you force a decision during this time, you won't be happy with the end result. Taking time for yourself is probably best. Sometimes when this card appears, it wants you to move from a space of logic and rational thinking to one of emotions. I also see this card for those who are focusing on mindfulness and meditation.

### Reversed

In its reversed position, the Two of Swords represents being stuck in limbo for way too long. People are waiting for you to make a decision and tell them what is going on, but you're refusing to do that right now. Either you don't know or telling the truth is too hard, so you'd rather say nothing at all. On the flip side, you may be refusing to take time out for yourself, so the decisions you're making are based upon temporary emotions. This card reversed indicates that this situation of being stuck in limbo is finally starting to shift.

There may be a moment of breakthrough, and you may be about to hear what you need to do next or find the answer you've been waiting for.

## THREE OF SWORDS

"I feel heartache and suffering."

Without a doubt, the Three of Swords is the card of disappointment and heartbreak. There's no way around this: You will experience a level of disappointment that feels like swords are ripping through your heart. This card represents emotional pain and feeling lost or abandoned. It seems as though you're in a dark space in your life, and you are being called to be patient with yourself and your own healing. You're in the thick of it now. When the Three of Swords appears, it is asking you to face the things that may feel uncomfortable but are necessary for your growth. This card gives you permission to cry and release emotions that may have been pent up. It's better to let it go than to hold on to that hurt and let it linger.

## Love

When the Three of Swords appears in matters of love, heartache or suffering is almost inevitable. If it's not new pain, this card points to facing old wounds and the ways they impact you in the present moment. There is the chance of some type of disappointing news or development that has the power to break your heart. You might be experiencing a breakup, discovering infidelity, or finding out that you or your partner is emotionally unavailable or checked out.

## Career/Work

The Three of Swords in a career/work-related reading indicates trouble in the workplace. No matter how you spin it, this card brings some level of heartache and disappointment. If there are changes going on in your career, chances are you're not happy about them. This card has a tendency to show up if you are about to lose your job or you are unsatisfied with your career choice or the direction your work path is taking you.

## Personal/Spiritual

In personal and spiritual readings, the Three of Swords has a tendency to fare better than in career or love readings. This is because, in this realm, we are more willing to work with hurt and understand it in order to transform. With this card, you are learning how to take your disappointment and grief and process them so that you can turn a negative situation into a positive. At the same time, we can't ignore that this card shows up when there is some type of suffering or stress that is happening now or is coming up. Changes around you may stem from your own heartache or may be leading into something that will be tough to deal with.

## Reversed

When reversed, the Three of Swords brings the pain to the next level. I don't want to trivialize anyone's suffering, but there are times when people allow their heartache to consume them to the point where it becomes worse than the original source of the pain. When the reversed Three of Swords shows up in a reading, something has broken your heart that should be over and done with but that continues to linger. For example, if there is a breakup and your partner hasn't moved out of the house—the breakup is bad enough, but now you have to think about it every time you look at them. What would have already been a stab to the heart now drags on and makes the pain significantly worse.

# FOUR OF SWORDS

## "I need to rest."

After the trauma of the Three of Swords, now we find rest. That is the energy of the Four of Swords. This card is the moment where you need to retreat and take time for yourself to restore your mind and body. For some, this may mean meditation or prayer; for others, it could be a vacation or something as simple as taking a nap. Either way, it's time to give yourself a chance to recover and get away from it all.

## Love

In love readings, the Four of Swords is a period of relaxation or retreat. You may be taking a break from your relationship or from dating right now to give yourself a rest. If you're in a relationship, you might be taking a temporary pause from each other or you may be going away as a couple—to a retreat or on a honeymoon—to get away from it all. This card is about time away for yourself, a time to find yourself so that, later, you can better connect with others. And simply because you need it.

## Career/Work

When the Four of Swords appears, you may be going on vacation or taking a pause from doing your work. This card often shows up for those who are going on sabbatical, changing their routine, or doing less than what they normally do, or for those who are forced from their job for whatever reason. I've also seen this card show up for those who are taking a moment of nonaction before starting a phase in their work life that requires a lot of energy. You may be preparing for what's to come, so you are pacing yourself and getting ready for the action, much the way retail employees might prepare ahead of time for the madness of the holiday rush. That calm phase is the Four of Swords in a nutshell.

## Personal/Spiritual

In spiritual and personal readings, the Four of Swords shows up for those who are taking a break away from it all because they need it. You may be going into prayer or meditation or needing to relax from your usual routine to gain clarity and direction in your life once again. Usually people feel refreshed and renewed once they allow themselves a Four of Swords type of moment. I often remind my clients how productive it is to take breaks. Remember, not all progress is good progress and not all movement forward is good movement forward. So taking a moment to regroup is more beneficial to your success than powering forward while feeling weak and drained and making a mess of all you worked so hard to accomplish.

### Reversed

When the Four of Swords shows up reversed, there are several potential outcomes. One is that you are stepping out of your break or your vacation feeling renewed and excited to get back into the swing of things once again. Another is that you have stayed out of commission for far too long. Finally, it could mean that you are refusing to take a break and are running on fumes. The energy of the number 4 is known to be stubborn—this is the negative aspect of the number revealing itself. For those who refuse to rest, the end result often tends to be disastrous.

## FIVE OF SWORDS

"I win! But at what cost?"

The Five of Swords is a card of brutal ego. This is where people want to win and achieve success, but they lose so much by making that their main focus. When this card appears, it's asking you if winning the battle is worth losing the entire war. People may end up getting their feelings hurt, and you may be sabotaging your own success and growth. The Five of Swords brings humility, embarrassment, and gloating. People are destructive, and they want revenge; they will do whatever they can to prove their points and gain power. You always want to be on the lookout when this card appears because it signifies an abundance of negative energy in the people and the environment around you.

### Love

In love readings, you really want to watch out when the Five of Swords appears. The people you are involved with are so consumed with their own egos and desires that there is no room for compromise or understanding. This is a relationship with someone who doesn't care about your feelings and may want to gain from you more than they could ever imagine giving. If you are single and this card appears for you, ask yourself in what ways you are self-sabotaging through learned negative behaviors and thoughts. With this card, people tend to act out for their own protection, but because the sword is double-edged, their actions can backfire. As much as you want love, you may end up isolating yourself and pushing others away because you refuse to be vulnerable or soft. You also may not know how to expect the best from others or yourself.

## Career/Work

When the Five of Swords appears, either someone in the workplace is working against you, or your own actions are destructive or selfish, and you are working against yourself. Your team will struggle to work together because people are butting heads rather than seeing one another's perspective. The differences between everyone are too great and the egos are so strong that they refuse to entertain another way of thinking. With this card, it seems like progress is minimal at best or bonds are broken or strained as a result of people's actions. Don't be surprised if you find out that someone is gossiping about you or actively trying to undermine you.

## Personal/Spiritual

When the Five of Swords appears in a personal or spiritual reading, you want to ask yourself honestly what ways you are self-sabotaging. Asking yourself that question is not easy, but with the Swords, you always have to be honest in order to grow. This suit doesn't care about your sensitive feelings; it cares about the truth. You may not want to see how you manipulate situations to get the end result you desire or how karma always has a way of catching up to you in the end.

## Reversed

When reversed, the negative energy of the Five of Swords has gone way too far. The level of gossip and revenge is extremely cold-blooded, and it impacts lives on a deeper level than it ever should. You or people around you are more than humiliated— their lives have been damaged as a result of what has been said and done. This card shows up reversed for people who are being bullied or who are bullies. Keep an eye out for people who are just looking for an attack or a fight—you will find them.

# SIX OF SWORDS

*"I'm learning that it's time to move forward and leave the past behind me."*

After the drama of the Five of Swords, we are finally moving forward with the Six of Swords, which represents exactly that: moving forward. You have picked up all there is to salvage of yourself and your self-respect, and you've clearly decided that enough is enough. You are moving into a (hopefully) more positive environment. With this card, your mind is essentially made up and you're done with the negative behaviors of the past. Getting away is good for you now and so is leaving any destructive behavior behind, as well as destructive people. Let them figure things out for themselves!

## Love

In love readings, the Six of Swords only shows up for people who have been through a lot mentally, emotionally, and spiritually. It makes more sense for them to move forward than for them to stay stuck in a negative or destructive situation. They're making these changes for the sake of their mind and heart, and that should not be ignored. If you decide to work out issues with your partner, the hope is that you two are journeying together to a far better place than the one you've left behind. The destructive ways of the past can't come forward with us as we move into the future. With this card, you are deciding to do things differently and to start fresh and new.

## Career/Work

In career readings, the Six of Swords indicates that you have decided—or maybe you've even been forced—to move on to the next stage on your journey. This is usually for the better, as you've been through a lot in the past and your focus now is on a brighter future. You have high hopes for this next phase of your life. Stress tends to ease and mellow out when the Six of Swords appears. I've also seen this card show up for those who work with people who are in recovery, are starting a new life, or are transitioning in life stages.

## Personal/Spiritual

The Six of Swords in your personal/spiritual life is about leaving your worries and your cares behind for the sake of your own well-being. This card usually hints at what you have gone through to get to where you are. It acknowledges your need for peace and a positive transition at this moment in your life. The number tends to soothe our worries temporarily, so this is important to understand when this card appears in your reading.

## Reversed

The journey into the next phase into your life is interrupted or even sabotaged when the Six of Swords appears reversed. You thought you were leaving your troubles in the past, but somehow, they managed to swim across the ocean and find you once again. If there was relief on the horizon, it now seems like it's either delayed or just not coming. On the other hand, you may be refusing to move forward in a situation because your heart is still stuck. This card is the universe suggesting that you need to let go. Swords always work with logical decision-making, but that's not always easy; the heart can overrule common sense. Either way, your journey forward is canceled, and you may need to confront your difficulties—or make a decision to let go—before you can move on.

## SEVEN OF SWORDS

*"Who can I trust?"*

This is the card that almost no one wants to see. The Seven of Swords is the card of cheating, deception, and stealing. It shows sneaky behavior and being robbed. It causes you to question your environment and the people within it and to ask yourself if you can really trust them. Should you do a little background search to find out who they are and what their motives could potentially be? In a more positive reading (which is rare with this card), the Seven of Swords can suggest relocation, but more often, it indicates that you'll want to find out if there is some sneaky, underhanded behavior going on around you.

## Love

Okay, yikes: The Seven of Swords suggests that the person you love or want to trust is simply not someone you can count on. You have to ask if someone is actually cheating or hiding something. Maybe someone is lying about their intentions or not telling you the whole truth. This doesn't always have to be negative. I have seen this card show up for people who have strong, deep feelings for another person but are hiding it because they are afraid to sabotage the entire relationship. But more often than not, this card shows up when someone—you or someone around you—is not speaking their truth, whatever that means for them.

### Career/Work
Anytime the Seven of Swords appears, you want to be a little extra careful than you normally would be. Swords deals with the mind and writing, so you want to be cautious about the words you're using: Someone could find a way to twist them and turn them against you. Also, someone you consider a friend or that you trust as a coworker may be sabotaging you in some way or waiting for their opportunity to stab a knife in your back. In a more positive reading, you may find yourself moving with your company if your workplace is relocating. Or you may simply run a moving company.

### Personal/Spiritual
This appearance of the Seven of Swords in a personal or spiritual reading hints that you may need to be honest with yourself and accept the truth of your current circumstance or behaviors. Again, the Swords wants to dish out the cold hard slap of truth, which

can be hard for most to digest. But just because it's difficult doesn't mean we should avoid it. Are you escaping from your own growth and healing and finding the easy way out? Lastly, you might need to question the intentions of those around you who are promising to help you. This card suggests that they may not be trustworthy.

### Reversed
With the Seven of Swords reversed, the truth has a way of finally coming out. You find out who or what has been working against you and maybe even why they were doing it in the first place. Maybe you'll get an apology, or what was taken from you may finally get returned. For example, let's say someone steals your wallet, a typical upright Seven of Swords moment. It's when the Seven of Swords shows up reversed that your wallet gets returned to you with your ID and your credit cards but with a $20 bill missing.

# EIGHT OF SWORDS

## "I am frozen in fear!"

The Eight of Swords will have you questioning your reality, paralyze you with fear, and leave you wondering who you can really trust. This is because if you take a step back and look at the Seven of Swords, someone or something at some point has lied or cheated and stolen from you. No wonder you're guarded and assuming the worst. The problem comes in when your own fears and anxieties stop you from inviting goodness into your life. When this card shows up, it signifies that sometimes our fears are worse than actual reality; you're guided to take off the blindfold and find your inner source of strength so you can see things for what they really are and feel empowered once again.

## Love

With the Eight of Swords in love readings, it feels practically impossible to trust and love again, and usually this is because you have gone through an incredible amount of pain. This card acknowledges your need for self-protection, but it is also trying to show you that your worst fears could really be your only enemy at this time. You may be finding yourself focusing on all the ways something can go wrong and ignoring all the ways something could go right. You may be questioning someone's motives or what is going to happen with the relationship or with your love life in general. Will you ever find love in this life? Is it a sign of cheating that your partner's coworker texted them at midnight? These are the questions that tend to surface when the Eight of Swords shows up within a love reading.

## Career/Work

Your fears are getting the best of you and stopping you from owning your power, being creative, and making clear logical decisions, as indicated by the Eight of Swords. You're expecting the worst and you have more fear than faith at this moment in time. It's possible your work environment has you powerless in some way. Perhaps you're waiting to hear an outcome, and you're paralyzed with anxiety because you don't know what to expect. When this card appears, we always think the worst is going to happen; you may even be questioning whether anything good can ever come. Because this card points to fear exaggerated, the outcome usually is not as bad as we thought it would be. But more than anything, this card represents a feeling of anxiety that has your stomach in complete knots.

### Personal/Spiritual

The Eight of Swords in personal and spiritual readings is a representation of how your thinking can get the best of you. As human beings, we tend to be highly intelligent and very imaginative. When this card appears, you're directing that smart and creative brain of yours to focus on all the ways something could go wrong. In what ways do you halt your own growth and hold yourself back? What is it that you're actually afraid of? These are the questions you need to ask when the Eight of Swords shows up in these types of readings.

### Reversed

When reversed, the Eight of Swords indicates that you have just enough confidence to peek beyond your blindfold and realize that your worst fears are just that—fears. It's not the fear that stopped you; it was you who decided to not move forward because you didn't know what was going to happen. This aha moment is the reversed Eight of Swords in a nutshell. You can now laugh at what used to hold you back. However, sometimes the energy of this card is heightened when reversed, and your anxiety may increase to the point of panic attacks, depression, or physical symptoms.

## NINE OF SWORDS

"My worst fears seem to be coming true . . ."

The Nine of Swords is another tough card found within the tarot. This card represents internal turmoil and stress that feels unbearable. It shows up for those who have spent nights and days worrying, losing sleep over whatever is causing them pain at the moment. The feelings of guilt are intense with this card. You feel hopeless, lost, and totally shaken by your own grief. You may be experiencing depression and paralyzing bouts of anxiety. I don't think I've ever seen this card show up in a way that was positive; so much internal suffering is connected with it.

### Love

In matters of love and relationships, the Nine of Swords often shows up for people who just experienced their worst fear happening.

Maybe you found out that the person you love betrayed you or maybe you've made a mistake you can't take back and it's eating you up inside. You may be facing situations or decisions that are too much for you to mentally handle right now. You are wishing that things were different or that someone will come in and save you or turn the outcome around. If you recently experienced a breakup, the mental anguish still lingers, and you're in need of some emotional support while you sort out your feelings. You are wondering if you will find love again. If you're in a relationship currently, you are suffering and looking for a way out or a solution to fix your romantic problem.

## Career/Work

With the Nine of Swords, the stress of your job has reached a place that is far too much for even the strongest to handle. You are worried about your workload, your security, stability, or what will happen in the future. The Nine of Swords can show up when you are agonizing over a decision you need to make. Something is really bothering you, and it may be completely outside your control. Maybe the struggle is mostly internal as you peer into your future with uncertainty. Where do I go and what do I do? These are the questions that can pop into your head when the Nine of Swords appears.

## Personal/Spiritual

The Nine of Swords in a personal reading reveals feelings of intense stress and anxiety. Oh, something is plaguing you and you can't seem to escape it. Physical pain can be numbed, but mental pain is something we can't really run away from. You're facing the reality of that right now. You may be feeling loveless, guilty, or hopeless, or maybe you're physically sick. Either way, this card indicates suffering, worry, and stress.

## Reversed

When the Nine of Swords appears reversed, the level of anxiety you're experiencing heightens tenfold. This is when your countless sleepless nights can make you feel like a zombie or out of touch with reality. It feels as though your worst fears keep manifesting and you're waiting for the next hit to come because you can sense something awful looming on the horizon. The anxiety is just too much to take, and you may find yourself having a total mental breakdown, needing help to guide you out of this dark place. Then again, when the Nine of Swords appears reversed, it can show that you may be exiting out of a highly stressful time and starting to see the light at the end of the tunnel. Maybe you've accepted your current situation, and it no longer gives you the same stress it once did. Sometimes, when this card appears reversed, it's showing up for a person who is almost resigned to their fate; what's happening no longer bothers them like it did when they originally faced it. Peace starts to set in.

## TEN OF SWORDS

"This is the end. We've hit rock bottom."

After the energy of the Nine of Swords, the Ten of Swords is a relief for many people. This is because you've finally hit rock bottom. You know what the worst outcome is because you just experienced it, and you can now start working on moving forward. The Ten of Swords is a card of total and complete endings. Usually when this card appears, you can't fix or repair what has happened; it is done. This is when you accept that you can't resurrect what has just ended, and in a weird way, it gives you peace. The end of the cycle has completed, the journey is over, and there's nowhere to go but up.

## Love

In love relationships, the Ten of Swords shows an ending. Sometimes this means a breakup or a split, but I've also seen this card show up for relationships that have been tested by outside circumstances. Finally, that cloud lifts so the couple is free to heal and move past what has happened. Whatever it is, you must let go of it because it is over. If you're single, this card could represent the end of singlehood and the start of a new relationship after a long period of not having someone to call your own. This card can also show up for someone who has completely given up hope and doesn't believe they will ever find love again. I can honestly say that it's usually that moment when all hope seems lost that everything has a way of miraculously falling together.

## Career/Work

The Ten of Swords in a work-related reading shows the end of a cycle. This could be spontaneous or something you knew was coming, but either way, you've reached the end of a stage within your career. If you are working toward a goal—for example, studying to pass quizzes or board exams— this is that moment when you take the test and submit it for review. All that you worked so hard for culminates in this very moment, and then it's time to say goodbye. You may be guided to walk away from a job, or you may even be facing retirement.

## Personal/Spiritual

When the Ten of Swords appears in personal readings, you want to be mindful of your thinking patterns and the energy they bring. Sometimes the Ten of Swords has the tendency to bring negative or worst-case-scenario thinking. If negative thinking is causing you suffering, it's time to say goodbye and release those thoughts because they don't serve you. It illustrates the ending of one phase in your life or the breakdown that creates the breakthrough for you to start over fresh. This card can be intimidating, but often the Ten of Swords appears to show you the blessing in a recent change you didn't choose. It reveals that there is strength to be gained by learning how to say goodbye.

## Reversed

The Ten of Swords reversed comes up when the universe is guiding you to say goodbye to something in your life that you refuse to let go of. This is that moment when something should end, but somehow it finds a way to keep lingering. Because the Ten of Swords brings such heavy feelings of sadness and disappointment, it can show up reversed for a person whose heartache is so unbearable that they need additional support to process it. Your faith may be tested, and you are questioning why this has happened. You can't seem to wrap your mind around it, which causes the pain to last even longer. In an otherwise positive reading, the swords found in this card are being pulled out of the person's back. As each sword is removed, there is a level of healing that occurs. You begin to understand why this change happened and that it truly was for the best.

# WANDS

**ASTROLOGICAL SIGNS:**
Aries, Leo, Sagittarius

**ELEMENT:** Fire

The Wands represent our passion and desires and are ruled by the element of fire. When these cards turn up in a reading, they represent excitement and the movement of energy, whether building up or dying down. These cards bring life, power, excitement, adventure, action, and even trouble! Working with this suit, you'll see a lot of red, yellow, and orange—all colors that represent fire energy.

# ACE OF WANDS

"I'm feeling the spark of passion and excitement!"

The Ace of Wands brings the spark of new life! Wands are connected to fire energy and your passions surge when this card turns up in your reading. You are starting some new adventure, and you are filled with intensity. Your optimism has increased, and you are fearless in the pursuit of your potential. You have the drive and ambition to do whatever it takes to make your dreams a reality. There is natural growth that occurs when the Ace of Wands appears in a spread. You are receiving exciting news, you are starting a brand-new adventure, or you are stepping out with faith into some new phase of your life.

## Love

When the Ace of Wands shows up in love readings, something has sparked your attraction and your attention. You feel the feverish desire to pursue a person you are drawn to like a moth to a flame. With the energy of the Wands, you'll need to be careful if you want a long-term relationship. This is because the Ace of Wands sparks interest quickly, but that spark can die out just as fast. When this card turns up, you are positively challenged to work toward attaining a goal for your relationship. You may be trying to win someone's heart because you see forever with them . . . but maybe it's just for one night.

## Career/Work

In work readings, the Ace of Wands indicates that you're feeling your ambition and passion now more than ever. This card shows up when something has challenged you and you are revving up to prove yourself and work toward your goal. This card often appears when you are starting some new journey, venture, or business and you are filled with ideas. You just can't wait to get started. You can use this energy and enthusiasm to gain attention and excitement around your idea and get others on board. Something big is starting within your work life and you're excited!

## Personal/Spiritual

For personal readings where the Ace of Wands shows up, you are being guided to connect with the things that excite you and ignite you. This card is about finding inspiration and adventure in your life once again. You might be called now to seek new ways to be challenged. This card shows up for people who are getting back into action after taking some time off or who need physical activity and stimulation in their life now. You can find yourself learning a new topic that you find fun and exciting, or maybe you're ready to expand your horizons and spontaneously book a ticket to a place you've never been and always wanted to visit. You've been bitten by the bug of adventure and are ready for exciting new experiences!

## Reversed

When reversed, the power and energy of the Ace of Wands is fizzled out. You've lost your mojo, you're no longer interested or attracted to what you once were, and what you thought would lift you off the ground just seems to completely poop out. People tend to be fickle and lose interest. This can be pretty frustrating to deal with because there had been so much excitement and adventure at the start, and then seemingly overnight it just died. The great adventure you saw for yourself feels squashed. Maybe someone in your life made a whole bunch of promises that now they can't keep. They talked a good game, but when it came down to it, they couldn't deliver.

# TWO OF WANDS

"What potential is out there for me?"

The Two of Wands is the card of potential. The symbolism of this card is usually a person who is holding a globe in their hand and looking out on the horizon, considering all their options. They realize that there is a whole world out there filled with things they have not yet discovered, and they are excited to get their hands on it and begin! The feelings of ambition, optimism, and curiosity are high with the Two of Wands. Whoever this is, they are excited to see what will develop. This person believes they have something special and worthy of sharing, and they're trying to connect with the right people to get what they envision off the ground.

## Love

In love readings, when the Two of Wands appears, it's common that you or someone around you is exploring their options or waiting for the perfect moment to approach a person they've had their eye on. There is a sense of restlessness and excitement that comes with this card because you can see the potential in the relationship or are excited to get back in the dating game once again. If you are currently in a relationship, it may be long-distance, or you are seeking new ways to rekindle its excitement and life. In otherwise negative relationship readings, we can't ignore the sense of passion that might be directed outside of a committed relationship. One of you could be secretly seeing what else is out there.

## Career/Work

With the Two of Wands, you are filled with ideas and want to collaborate with others to create something special, especially when it comes to networking and problem-solving. You might have international clients or work that has you traveling and connecting with people outside your office. The Two of Wands is always looking out beyond what is right in front of you. It feels like the potential ahead is limitless, and you are excited to see what will develop when you get the right people on your side to help you build this great vision. This card signifies the early stages of planning and development—the potential is there, but only time will tell what will actually cement and develop.

## Personal/Spiritual

In spiritual and personal readings, the Two of Wands is guiding you to ask for more for yourself. The Two of Wands shows up when you are ready to grow, connect, and explore, and you are reviewing all your options. You are asking yourself, "What gifts could this world have to offer and what can I give in return?" You are ready to get out there and see where this new life path can take you. You might find yourself being called to travel or to get involved with group activities that spark your interest and passion.

## Reversed

When reversed, the Two of Wands indicates a situation where you once saw potential but now feel like nothing can come from it. You're having a hard time getting others to believe in your vision or maybe you're feeling shy and scared to take that first step. Often, when this card appears, you may be trying to bite off more than you can chew; getting the ball rolling ends up being much harder than you expected. You might find yourself wanting to give up. Networking and connecting with others are proving to be way more difficult than you anticipated—maybe because not everybody is on the same page or has the same vision. The trip you wanted to take might be canceled or delayed for now.

## THREE OF WANDS

*"Waiting for the results to come in!"*

Finally! When the Three of Wands appears in your reading, you have not only gotten the ball rolling with your ideas, but it seems like a positive result is actually approaching in the near future. There is a lot of activity happening around you, as others are willing to work together to see your project through and help it grow. You've made the right connections, and they are coming through with their resources. You've taken your first step in initiating this new venture or project, and the excitement is high as you're watching things continue to unfold.

## Love

With the Three of Wands in love readings, you have a sense that the energy you put out is now starting to come back to you. Maybe you've gone on a successful date with someone you like and they've said they want to see you again, but you're waiting for the actual details of time and place to come through. Because the Three of Wands is connected to overseas, you might find yourself in a relationship that's exclusively or mostly online, maybe even long-distance. This card is always looking out into the horizon to find its happiness. If you're in a relationship right now, you and your partner may be looking toward the future with high hopes and expectation; you may feel that what you've built so far will be a success.

## Career/Work

In a work and career reading, the Three of Wands shows you that something has lifted off the ground and you're waiting for the results and the reward. Just like in a general reading, you've somehow managed to find the right connections to support your business or work. There is a lot of activity with new clients and financial growth, and it's unbelievably exciting! You're filled with ideas and you're open to any challenge that comes your way. For you, this stage in your work life is more than an idea—it's actually producing tangible results. It's laying the foundation for all that is to come.

## Personal/Spiritual

The Three of Wands in a personal reading is guiding you to explore new areas of growth and potential that you normally wouldn't have considered. This card could be calling you to travel or to connect with others to consider different ideas that could spark inspiration within you and give your life more meaning and substance. You are excited for your future and what is to come because you've initiated some adventures you've been wanting to explore for some time. If you are interested in personal growth, this card shows up when you don't just talk about the new classes and the new activities you're curious about—you actually sign up and go do them. It's easier said than done, but so worth it!

## Reversed

When reversed, the Three of Wands brings disappointment and frustration because, where you thought a new venture or project was a sure deal, it's now experiencing blockages and delays. For whatever reason, this idea you thought you could achieve effortlessly requires more energy than you were expecting it to. Others can't hold their end of the bargain, leaving you hanging high and dry. Maybe the excitement you originally started off with is dying down or the attraction starts to dissipate. You might be deciding if you should continue this pursuit or if it's best just to direct your attention elsewhere.

# FOUR OF WANDS

*"Pop the champagne! We have something major to celebrate!"*

The Four of Wands is the card of celebration, coming home, and building a secure foundation of love and pleasure! Life has brought you to a major milestone moment that you are grateful to celebrate. This card is about establishing roots for yourself, having supportive people around you, and being proud of what you've worked so hard to achieve. You've not only started to see your initial ideas come to fruition, you can now trust that this good luck will continue to bring you even more rewards!

## Love

The Four of Wands brings commitment and stability to a relationship. Sometimes this means making the relationship exclusive between you and someone you love—perhaps choosing to marry or build a home. The number 4 within the tarot and numerology always bring a solid foundation to support the rest of your journey, and that's what the Four of Wands brings to you now. You are not only happy but are also celebrating important accomplishments or milestones with friends and family. This card has a strong connection to our relationships with people we truly love, care for, and admire.

## Career/Work

In work-related readings, the Four of Wands brings a moment to celebrate your hard work! Usually this is that moment where you sign a lucrative deal with a client or you get a promotion you've been working hard to attain. This card brings success, feelings of accomplishment, and a sense of security for yourself. You feel comfortable in this phase of your life but also hopeful about your own future. This card is almost always positive and promises good feelings all around.

## Personal/Spiritual

The Four of Wands in a personal reading represents that warm sensation of "coming home"—seeing the people you love and celebrating the things you are most grateful for. You're at a place in your life where you are provided for and happy with how far you've come. You might find that you're buying a house or solidifying a business you have put your heart and soul into building, or maybe you're finding yourself going on a vacation with people who are ready to have a good time! This card wants you to enjoy yourself and the present moment. You've earned it.

### Reversed

When the Four of Wands is reversed, there's still the potential to set your roots down, but it comes with a delay. If you are buying a house and you had your eyes on something specific, someone else might have put in a larger offer and you might have to settle for your second-best option. In relationships, you and your partner have made a commitment to each other, but for whatever reason, it doesn't provide as much joy as you thought it would. Maybe it comes with a compromise of some sort. If you are going on a vacation, maybe it rains the entire time; if you're celebrating with family, maybe your favorite aunt is missing from the gathering. When this card shows up reversed, there's still a chance to celebrate, but it's not as perfect as you would have liked it to be. This card reminds you to celebrate the moment regardless.

## FIVE OF WANDS

"I need to prove myself!"

When the Five of Wands appears, you feel you need to prove something. Either you are fighting for attention or fighting for the sake of a challenge. Maybe the competition around you is strong and you need to learn how to be assertive and dominant to get what you want. Wand energy is ruled by fire, so you are going feel the effects of your passion, drive, and ambition. This card may show up when you are butting heads with someone and can't seem to agree or get along. But you can use this moment to respectfully show others what you're really made of.

### Love

The Five of Wands shows that you have competition around you in matters of love. Perhaps the person you have your eyes on or that you love is distracted by something in their environment like work-related responsibilities or other people they may be dating or paying attention to. Either way, it feels like you're fighting for them to spend quality time with you and take you seriously. You may also be butting heads with your partner in a way that can start off as play fighting but quickly turn into something more serious. This could be as simple as two people arguing over who's going to cook dinner or do the dishes—ha ha!—but the energy of proving yourself and winning the argument is definitely there. It may start out in good fun and turn into a real argument.

## Career/Work

The Five of Wands appears when you are trying to compete with others or argue your point of view. For example, if you are a lawyer and you're fighting to defend your client, it's your job to present enough evidence to win the case despite any opposing theories or evidence. In other career-related readings, you're fighting to prove that you are the one most worthy of achieving your goal. This could be a promotion or a new title you've been working toward with great ambition. You might also be in a heavy negotiating or brainstorming session that brings a lot of energy to your meeting; everyone is working toward a common goal by trying to create something catchy and exciting.

## Personal/Spiritual

The Five of Wands in a personal reading invites a little healthy competition into your life. This could be as literal as signing up for a fencing class or some other type of competitive sport to release pent-up frustrations, get exercise, and meet like-minded people. This card encourages you to be assertive and to accept challenges to discover your own potential to compete. This is not a time to give up but to push yourself to see what exactly you can do—of course, without hurting yourself or anyone else in the process. You might be setting goals and working daily to achieve them. Sometimes your only competition is yourself, but you still want to prove to yourself how strong you are and what you can accomplish.

## Reversed

When the Five of Wands shows up reversed, your obstacles may turn out to be a little bit more challenging than what you were expecting. You may need to put in a little extra work to show up and win the argument or achieve the goal you've set your heart on. Someone around you may have one up on you; it's a small blow to your ego a to watch them win. Sometimes—with this card reversed—people end up gloating about their wins to the point where it becomes unhealthy and hurtful. On the flip side, you may give up halfway through because you don't like the feeling of competing with others, or you feel insecure about what you can do.

# SIX OF WANDS

"I win!"

The Six of Wands is the card of success, accomplishments, and recognition. This is that moment when you feel like a celebrity; people are cheering you on and celebrating you for your gifts. Usually, when this card appears, you love this attention; you've worked so hard to achieve your goals, and having people recognize you validates all the effort you put in. It's absolutely worth it, even if it's just for this moment. You are receiving encouragement, rewards, and attention, and you are soaking it up!

## Love

In a love relationship reading, the Six of Wands has you feeling like you're on top of the world! You may have just had a first kiss with a new love, have just said yes to a proposal, or found someone you are so excited about that you can't even believe your luck! When this card appears, it encourages you to tell people how much you appreciate them and to use positive reinforcement to let them know what they're doing right. In a negative reading, the Six of Wands can hint toward a person who is a little overconfident in their abilities to make you happy and fulfilled. Or maybe it's you who needs a little bit of an ego check.

## Career/Work

The Six of Wands brings success, reward, and acknowledgment. In work-related readings, this card usually points to a promotion or some type of upgrade in your work situation. If you are in college, this is that moment where you're walking down the aisle to receive your diploma. You're feeling on top of the world and proud of all the work that got you to this point.

## Personal/Spiritual

In readings focused around spirituality and personal growth, the Six of Wands encourages you to focus on positive thinking and your desired outcome. This card uses the laws of attraction to call in the accomplishment and rewards you are seeking in your life now. You are aware of your strengths as well as your weaknesses, and you are applying this understanding to your own personal growth. You are beginning to feel like you're on top of the world, celebrating this higher level of self-confidence, self-love, and self-worth! Maybe you receive a reward or recognition for your contributions to a group or society. This is a proud moment you'll remember for the rest of your life!

## Reversed

The Six of Wands reversed represents a reward you should receive that, for some reason, doesn't appear. You've worked so hard to prove yourself or to fight for others, but when all is said and done, it feels like a letdown. Maybe people don't appreciate or see the good you have done for them or maybe along the journey you've lost something or someone important to you; the success may feel empty at best. In other readings, this card shows up reversed for people with low self-esteem who are hungry for fame and just can't seem to get enough of others telling them how good they are. Either way, it feels like the success you should be celebrating is not enough.

"I need to protect myself."

When the Seven of Wands appears within a reading, you may feel defensive or on edge. You are struggling to prove yourself and are under a lot of pressure and stress, but you still don't want to give up. Not yet. The Seven of Wands brings courage and a need to prove yourself, so you'll do whatever it takes to fight the good fight despite the odds. People might be telling you to give up because winning seems impossible, but something within you has ignited your fighter spirit, and you're not going down easily. Your strength and courage are at an all-time high, and even if you are scared, you're not going to show it because you have something to prove. You are confident in yourself and your abilities.

## Love

The Seven of Wands in love relationships can symbolize a couple working really hard on their relationship. As in other readings, it may seem like the odds are stacked against them, but they refuse to give up. There's something about the relationship they want to fight for. If you're single, maybe you've been struggling to find someone you're attracted to, but you're not going to stop trying. In fact, you may try even harder than usual because this is something you really want for yourself and you feel like there's something more out there waiting for you. I've often seen this card show up for people who are attempting to prove to someone that they are worthy of their love, affection, and attention. Sometimes it works and sometimes it doesn't, but either way, they're not giving up anytime soon.

## Career/Work

The Seven of Wands reveals that you are determined to succeed and move beyond present obstacles. You may be negotiating for the sake of your business—perhaps to lower operation costs to increase profits. Or you may have to prove that you have what it takes to succeed; you are rolling up your sleeves to tackle some challenging career problem. Not only do you believe in yourself and in your abilities, but you are also fighting to protect something you truly have faith in. You won't go down without a fight. The challenge you're facing may be difficult, but you have what it takes to turn this negative into a positive—and that's exactly what you'll do.

## Personal/Spiritual

The Seven of Wands in personal readings represents a phase in your life where you are called to find out exactly what you are made of. You have to call on your inner strength and determination to move beyond your present challenges for the sake of your own growth. You are beginning to believe in yourself and your gifts and learning to work with your weaknesses so that you can become stronger. Your faith may be tested at this time, but at the end of it, there is always a reward!

## Reversed

You're starting to question yourself when the Seven of Wands shows up reversed within a reading. Originally you thought you had what it takes to win and move past this challenge, but the opposition seems stronger than you were originally expecting. A part of you may feel like you need to give up, and you may ask yourself, "Why am I trying so hard to prove myself?" Sometimes when the Seven of Wands reversed shows up, this card is suggesting that maybe you should back down. But your ego has been ignited and you can't let go of the fight, even though this could be to your detriment. There is a slightly higher chance you will lose this battle than you expected, and it's up to you to decide: Is it worth it to continue? Or should you back down, even if it might be a blow to your ego?

# EIGHT OF WANDS

*"Everything is moving so fast!"*

The Eight of Wands always brings speed, action, and activity. This is the card of things coming in and going out and all very quickly! Usually this card brings excitement, news, or the possibility of spontaneous adventure because it is always on the go! When the Eight of Wands appears, you know something is going to come dashing in, requiring a quick yes or no. And more often than not, it's a yes! This card represents communication, things that bring high energy, and the chance to move forward into a new beginning sooner rather than later.

## Love
When the Eight of Wands appears, you can expect a speedy romance. Maybe you'll soon cross paths with an unexpected person who will spark passion in your life; maybe it's something as simple and specific as speed dating. If you're waiting to hear from someone you love, you can expect to get a call or text from them shortly. In fact, check your phone right now—it may have already come in! That is how fast the energy of this card is! In established relationships where you are working to take your commitment to the next level, this card may allow you to begin conversations that will inform you where this relationship is headed. The energy of the Wands suit typically brings excitement. The messages you receive when you pull this card tend to get your heart racing.

## Career/Work
With the Eight of Wands, you may find yourself negotiating with a client or traveling for work-related events. This card is always on the go and filled with energy, so that's what you can expect when it appears in a reading. Things move fast around you, so you need to be ready to keep up or you will be quickly left behind! If you are waiting for a good idea to pop into your head, it will happen when you least expect it. If you have experienced any delays in the past, they are clearing now—you are ready to move forward.

## Personal/Spiritual
The Eight of Wands in personal/spiritual readings is pushing you to be bold, leave stagnant situations that are holding you back, and charge forward confidently in the direction of your dreams! This card craves excitement and adventure, and it doesn't

want to stay in a space that feels boring or that sucks all the life and creativity out of you. You may be called to make quick decisions in some area of your life now. This is that moment when a friend texts you that they have booked two tickets to Paris this weekend, and you immediately say yes to the adventure!

## Reversed

When the Eight of Wands is reversed, the message or phone call you were hoping to receive has been intercepted. Some kind of delay is stopping you from speeding forward. This card can often show up for people who like the idea of adventure more than actually living it out, so they will say no to something instead of hopping onboard spontaneously. What you thought was a clear sign for yes turns out to be a no. Plans cancel, energy feels wasted, and there are problems with travel.

# NINE OF WANDS

*"I am so exhausted."*

When the Nine of Wands appears in your reading, you are feeling beyond exhausted. Life seems to have beaten you up and now you find yourself feeling defensive. Because of everything you have gone through, you can be triggered by even the smallest things. Yet even when the Nine of Wands appears, you're still not going to tap out, no matter how much you want to. There's still something left to fight for, and that's exactly what you plan to do.

## Love

In love readings, the Nine of Wands represents the moment where you take your last stand. You're not ready to walk away from the relationship, but everything you've gone through with each other has worn you and/or your partner down. Your guard is still up and you're defensive, but you haven't given in yet. People who are single may be protecting their heart and feeling very wary of letting someone in at this point. You really want love and you're not going to give up in your quest to find it, but at the same time, it's exhausting and you're wondering what's going to come of this.

## Career/Work

The Nine of Wands is the card of the fighter and the advocate. You are battling for a cause because it's something you believe in, and despite the obstacles, you're not ready to give up or give in. When this card appears in a work-related reading, it's usually because you have put in long hours at the office working on a project and you can see the finish line, but there's still so much that remains to be done. If you're running a business, this is that phase in your journey where all your responsibilities are wearing you down, but you are determined to see things through till the end. There may be a lot of changes in your career right now and you're not sure what's going to happen, but you're not going to walk away from your job now. If anything, you're going to fight harder for it.

## Personal/Spiritual

In readings centering on spirituality and personal growth, your willpower and determination are being tested right now. Personally, you may be feeling worn down and in need of recovery time. If you've been working a lot lately on self-improvement and your personal goals, it may be time for you to take a break for the sake of your own well-being. You know you have what it takes to be successful, but it's also okay for you to take a moment for yourself so that you can rebuild your strength. Every day doesn't have to be a struggle. Do something nice for yourself—you deserve it!

## Reversed

When the Nine of Wands shows up reversed, the opposition is closing in and you're feeling like you're going to get swallowed up or defeated. You've done all you can to prove yourself, and somehow it doesn't feel like it's enough. Maybe in your exhaustion you've had a moment of weakness or distraction—something catches you off guard—and that's the straw that breaks the camel's back. This card, when reversed, shows you that your health and well-being may actually be at risk and that you may be better off asking for help or even tapping out. What you originally thought was worth fighting for may be a lost cause or just not worth it at this time.

# TEN OF WANDS

"The weight I'm carrying is a heavy one . . . "

The Ten of Wands is the card of not giving up no matter how heavy the burden is! This card shows up when you are tired and overwhelmed, but you remain determined to do whatever it takes to make it to the finish line. Your commitment to this cause is admirable. Your tasks and responsibilities are time-consuming, but you're not afraid of hard work. You are ambitious, and your will to succeed is what is fueling you now. This card shows up when you refuse to give up!

## Love

In love and relationship readings, the Ten of Wands indicates that you are at a place in your life where you realize that it's not always going to be easy. Every day may seem like a struggle, but you're not going to give up on the person you love. If you're single, you may have a lot on your plate right now, but you're still somehow finding time for dating. You may have gone through a lot in your past, but your hope that you will find someone special is carrying you forward.

## Career/Work

Your responsibilities at work are weighing heavily on your shoulders now. Maybe more work is being placed on your desk, and it's your job to sort through it all and get the task done. It's really important to monitor the amount of stress you are placing on yourself; carrying the weight of the Ten of Wands for too long in any area of your life is a lot for anybody to handle and can be detrimental to your actual health and well-being. This card can also show up for people who work manual labor jobs that are very physically demanding. Regardless, this card represents your ambition and your determination despite the obstacles of opposition.

## Personal/Spiritual

The Ten of Wands in a personal reading represents the responsibilities and commitment you're currently carrying. Maybe it's not actual work: Guilt or expectations you have for yourself or others can weigh you down emotionally or mentally over time, too. You may not even realize that you're carrying this burden on your heart because you've become so accustomed to the way this weight feels. This card asks you to look at what you are holding on to and examine if it's worth it to carry it forward into the future, or if you're better off letting it go.

## Reversed

When reversed, the Ten of Wands is way too heavy for you to carry; you are collapsing under its weight. The responsibilities and expectations are too much; you can't do this alone, nor should you be expected to. You have overworked yourself, and your stress has skyrocketed. It's time to ask for help. Sometimes when this card is reversed you have willingly accepted more than you should have, and it's starting to catch up to you. When this card appears reversed in health-related readings, you need to spend time rebuilding your strength so that you can fight off whatever it is that is making you feel weak or ill. It's okay to ask for help.

# 5

# THE COURT CARDS

**F THE MAJOR ARCANA REVEAL LIFE'S BIG LESSONS** and the Minor Arcana are concerned with its more mundane day-to-day details, the Court Cards represent the people and messengers that populate your life. Just like in the Minor Arcana, the Court Cards are broken down into different suits, organized around the four elements—water (Cups), fire (Wands), earth (Pentacles), and air (Swords). Each elemental group has a page, knight, queen, and king, who all bring their own levels of maturity and growth to the reading. No matter what the element, pages and knights tend to manifest most often as young people, immature energy, or messengers, while the king and queen represent greater maturity—whether it be reality or by intention. Let's look at each card in turn.

# CUPS

## PAGE OF CUPS

"I am the dreamer, the artist, the poet, and the romantic. Let's create art together."

The Page of Cups is the youngest and most immature of the Cups Court Cards. It represents the budding of new feelings, creativity, romance, and love. Because these feelings are so new, the Page of Cups is equal parts innocent and vulnerable. You will find him to be shy, introverted, or bashful as he explores what he's feeling while influenced by the spell of the first waves of love. This card signifies that moment when you have butterflies in your stomach or a crush on someone for the first time in a long time. You may be receiving an offer or invitation to go on a date or to a party or event, or you may receive a loving note or text from a friend. Because the Page of Cups is a messenger card, he usually brings news with him, so don't be shocked if you do receive a text or phone call from someone you love. This may be an invitation to talk or go out, especially to an artistic event or to meet for a walk in the park. This card brings tenderness, sweetness, and good emotion, so it tends to be more positive than anything.

### Love

The Page of Cups hints that the first signs of love or affection are beginning to grow! When this card appears in a reading, you usually will find that you have your eye on someone, see them as sweet or caring, or are at the beginning stages of new love. You may be asked out on a date, find yourself sharing sweet and tender moments with someone new, or telling someone you love them for the first time. As sweet as this card is, we can't ignore the fact that the Page of Cups is connected to emotions of all kinds—and not just the emotions that make you feel all warm and fuzzy inside. You may have something heavy that has been sitting on your heart that you need to express through words or writing.

## Career/Work

The Page of Cups appears when a job offer or proposal is somewhere on the horizon! Because it is connected closely to the arts and creative works, those aspects can show up in your career life now. This card can also easily represent a person who is new and shy to the job—maybe you are in charge of looking after this person, or maybe you are the one who is in training or being guided. The Page of Cups encourages you to follow your intuition and be gentle with yourself and others.

## Personal/Spiritual

The Page of Cups is one of the most powerful signifiers of sensitive people, empaths, and developing intuitives. The gifts he brings may be misunderstood by some people—he may not seem to fit in at first—but as he grows older and more mature, his unusual talents will work to help heal others, especially through new age medicine, psychic energy work, or counseling. When this card appears in your reading, these aspects of healing are good for you now. You'll also see this card when you are working with journaling, writing, painting, and creating music or art. You may need a retreat to escape from the harshness of the world.

## Reversed

When the Page of Cups is reversed, it is absolutely heartbreaking. This is because upright he is so filled with optimism, love, and potential. When he appears reversed, something has totally popped his bubble and he's lost in his own heartbreak. If someone has given you something, they are now taking it away. You are a lost lamb; the light of your love still burns, but it seems all hope is lost. Depression and sadness can settle in, and, as you mourn, you will cry or maybe just feel totally off balance. The reversed Page of Cups is an invitation taken away and the first sting of heartbreak.

# KNIGHT OF CUPS

KNIGHT of CUPS.

"I'd love to offer this gift to you . . . "

The Knight of Cups is your knight in shining armor! He has been guided by his heart and intuition to find what he loves no matter the obstacle or cost. He will do whatever it takes because, in his eyes, there is nothing more important than winning the heart of someone you love or pursuing your truest desires. The Knight of Cups brings the energy of the hopeless romantic: the seed of love and inspiration that is growing or the invitation to escape to paradise. All of the pages and knights act as messengers, and the Knight of Cups is the one who brings news connected to the heart, feeling, and intuition. You are being guided by your heart—even if its path doesn't make sense. This is not just in romantic relationships, although that is common with this card, but in all things that hold a high emotional value for you.

## Love

When the Knight of Cups appears in a love reading, here again we see signs of the hopeless romantic. This is the phase in your life where your heart is pulled toward someone or someone is being pulled toward you. Because he is a messenger, the Knight of Cups usually represents someone asking for a date or trying to move the relationship forward in some sweet and meaningful way (*ahem*, a proposal!). The chances of meeting a handsome stranger and falling in love increase when this card appears. Invitations to social events or gatherings are things you should say yes to now, especially if you are single and looking—and your intuition tells you to!

## Career/Work

Some new experience or offering is swirling in the cosmos for you when the Knight of Cups appears in a career reading. This knight enjoys a night out, a party, social events, and a beautiful vacation . . . especially one spent near a lake or ocean. In other readings, you could find yourself using your intuition to guide you to say yes or no to new projects. The Knight of Cups is very much a dreamer, so it's possible that you are pursuing some kind of project that may seem impossible or difficult for others but not for you—you are intuitively guided and will pursue it to satisfy and fulfill your heart.

## Personal/Spiritual

You have full permission to lose yourself in your imagination, in love, and/or in your art when the Knight of Cups appears. It's hard not to when you are the under the spell of this knight. Your intuition and heart are guiding you toward places you could only dream of—your imagination runs away with you! There is a dream or vision you've had for yourself—maybe a new life or experience— that you are currently feeling called to. To you, it's so beautiful that you have stars in your eyes as you imagine all that can happen! The Knight of Cups is the card of the impossible romantic dream that you now have the potential to make reality.

## Reversed

Just like the Page of Cups, when the Knight of Cups is reversed, he usually symbolizes a tough heartbreak or news that disappoints. He can represent a person whose intentions and motives need to be questioned. He may seem romantic but could really just be saying anything he needs to in order to sweep you off your feet for the moment. It's pretty reckless what can tumble out of his mouth, so you'll need to listen to your intuition. If something feels off, it most likely is. When reversed, the Knight of Cups brings disillusionment more than anything solid or concrete. Perhaps its intentions are not evil, but this card reversed is emotionally out of balance; the nature of invitations you are receiving is flaky at best and shouldn't be taken too seriously. Another thing to look out for is someone near you abusing drugs or alcohol—the Knight of Cups reversed has a strong need to escape from reality. He just can't deal with the real world, so he'll find any way he can to keep his head in the clouds.

## QUEEN OF CUPS

QUEEN of CUPS.

"I am the queen of compassion and I'll nurture you back to health."

This is the soft, nurturing mother of the tarot deck. Of all the queens, the Queen of Cups is the most connected to her emotions. She is highly psychic and exudes nurturing vibes even when she's not trying. She's the person who can tell that something is off even if you have convinced everyone else that you are okay. She senses it and will wait until you are alone to sit you down, pour you some tea, and ask again. Something about her feels safe, and you know you are protected and cared for in her presence; you can tell her your secrets and know she will listen and support you and help you feel better once again. She knows the right words to say. She is also an amazing listener and will give you the best hugs—ones you didn't even know you needed! She is naturally empathetic, affectionate, and can nurse most things back to life with loving care.

## Love

In love readings, the Queen of Cups represents a person who is connected to their emotions and finds themselves being drawn to take care of and nurture others. This person usually loves children or spending time with family and kids. They are soft-spoken, kindhearted, and love healthy partnerships. When this card shows up in a reading, it's either referencing the person asking the question or it's saying you'll benefit from bringing that energy into your love life. Be kind to others, ask them how they are feeling, and connect with your own feelings. Intuition tends to be heightened at this time, so be sure to listen to your gut instinct if something feels off.

## Career/Work

Who does the Queen of Cups represent in your workplace? This is someone who will play an important role in your career now. Or it may be that you are the one exuding her traits. In either case, this card is connected with patience and understanding, or you may find yourself providing consultations to others. You are drawn to careers involving psychology, healing, nursing, or caretaking roles. You can thrive in your career if you are able to work with your intuitive gifts and use new age practices of healing. The Queen of

Cups is the one most likely to work from home or to be a homemaker of some sort.

## Personal/Spiritual

In readings revolving around your personal life or spiritual well-being, the Queen of Cups is a guide or guru who appears to you in your physical life or in the spiritual realm. She provides emotional support and works to teach you to develop your intuitive and psychic senses. Instead of fighting against your sensitivities, you want to work with them because they show you what your body is resonating with and what it is rejecting. The appearance of the Queen of Cups is a reminder to nurture yourself as much as you would nurture others. You need you, too. Be easy on yourself, be gentle with others, and don't be afraid to talk about your feelings or write them down and share them.

## Reversed

When the Queen of Cups shows up reversed, she has a tendency to use emotion to manipulate others to get what she wants. Maybe she doesn't know she is doing this, but either way, it's happening. The Queen of Cups reversed may also represents a person who is emotionally clingy and very needy at this point in her life. She may be struggling with allowing others to make decisions for themselves and even with making decisions for her. Her self-esteem may be low, and her self-worth has plummeted, so her decision-making is questionable. She is weak, at least for the moment.

## KING OF CUPS

KING of CUPS.

"I am the king you can trust and count on to be there when you need a friend."

The King of Cups is a card that represents emotional stability. He is in tune with his feelings naturally and effortlessly. He's not afraid to express his love to the people he cares about, and those around him know him to be caring, considerate, patient, and compassionate. He's the friend you can go to if you need advice, but he also maintains healthy boundaries between himself and others. He's intuitive (though maybe not as intuitively gifted as the Queen of Cups) and has somewhat of a psychic sense. The King of Cups is a natural nurturer and is always kind to whomever he crosses paths with. Usually he has a smile on his face and is quick to show his approval and support for the people he meets.

### Love
In matters of love, the King of Cups represents someone who knows exactly what they want in a relationship, and they are usually looking for a companion who is equally solid, compassionate, and loving. The King of Cups is affectionate and nurturing; he is not afraid of intimacy. In fact, he likes it and needs it! Words of affirmation and touch are his love language. If this is someone you are currently in love with, there's a good chance he is someone you can trust with your heart, but you still need to give him time to develop solid feelings—the moments you spend together will help with this. As much as he would like a relationship, he's not one to rush into something without first feeling intuitively guided that this is the right person for him at this time in his life. Once he enters into a relationship, he will give it his all, and the connection will be one that is romantic and filled with love and support.

### Career/Work
With regard to work, the King of Cups represents a knowledgeable person in the office you can approach for advice and guidance without feeling like an idiot for asking. He is always encouraging, supportive, and friendly toward others, and his door is open to those who need him. Most people respect and feel comfortable around him. He's also pleasant

and responsible. The King of Cups is someone whose intentions are usually good, but he has a tendency to be late to meetings and sometimes can get distracted or be a bit disorganized. People love him regardless.

## Personal/Spiritual

The King of Cups asks you to connect with your heart's true desires and to take them seriously. When this card shows up, you are being asked to create emotional balance and stability in your life. You don't want to rush into things; rather, give them time to develop. This is the wisdom the King of Cups brings. This card's appearance reminds you to be there for others and for yourself but also to learn how to establish healthy boundaries to protect your own emotional well-being. You may be a highly sensitive person, but you need to learn how to better take care of yourself so that you don't take on too much of other people's burdens or the weight of the world.

## Reversed

You want to be very mindful when the King of Cups shows up reversed. He tends to manipulate and say all of the right things to get what he wants. When reversed, the king is no longer mature; he will look for any way to escape from reality because he can't deal with the harshness this world can sometimes bring. When the King of Cups is reversed, sometimes we see alcoholism, drug addiction, or escape through sex or fantasy. This person is not to be trusted and will deceive you. If this is someone you are in a relationship with, you might even find stalker tendencies if you decide to break up. He simply cannot let go, and he'll never want to say goodbye.

# PENTACLES

## PAGE OF PENTACLES

PAGE of PENTACLES.

"I am the messenger of patience, study, and resourcefulness."

The Page of Pentacles shows up when patience, determination, and hard work are starting to take center stage in your life. Just like the other pages, this one often appears as a messenger. Because the Pentacles are connected to earth energy and material manifestation, you may be receiving news about your work, money/finances, or projects you have committed yourself to. For the Page of Pentacles, slow and steady pays off over time, not overnight.

## Love

When the Page of Pentacles appears, you are starting to consider whether you can commit to the person in your life. There's something in them that you find worthy and you want to take the relationship more seriously and explore where it could potentially go. Also, when this card appears, it's a flag to take your time getting to know this person in order to build the relationship. There is no rush when this card appears; in fact, the Page of Pentacles believes that slow and steady truly does win the race. In readings where a partnership has already been established, the couple is working together to build a foundation for the next phase of their life together. It feels positive and real because both people are equally committed to each other and the future they're working toward.

## Career/Work

In career and work-related readings, when the Page of Pentacles appears, you are at the beginning stages of creating a solid foundation for your business or your work life. You are finding it easy to dedicate yourself to a work-related goal, and you are devoted to learning all you can. You are applying your energy to doing research and securing resources to help your business grow. The Page of Pentacles is committed and takes himself seriously in his work life. There is still much to learn and do at this current stage, but the potential is there; others are most likely taking notice and are willing to invest in you.

### Personal/Spiritual

When the Page of Pentacles appears with regard to your personal or spiritual life, you are learning how to be patient with yourself and with others. A firm foundation can't be rushed; some things are better developed over time versus overnight. You are in a phase in your life where you are doing research—possibly learning or working as an apprentice under someone who is sharing their knowledge with you. You are interested in what you're studying; it requires your diligence and full attention. To be successful, you need to be committed.

### Reversed

When the Page of Pentacles shows up reversed, we see someone whose commitment is lacking; maybe they're feeling lazy, and they're starting to take shortcuts. In business- or work-related readings, the finances necessary to create a solid foundation for your dream are lacking. In relationships, a commitment you made is now being called into question; someone wants all of the reward without putting in any work. Oftentimes, the Page of Pentacles reversed shows that someone may

committed but is so focused on the tiny details that they can't move forward. They may be stuck over things they should just accept and let go of.

## KNIGHT OF PENTACLES

KNIGHT of PENTACLES.

"I am dedicated to learning and growing."

The Knight of Pentacles represents progress that is steady, consistent, and building every single day. You or others are committed to a goal, and the hard work is beginning to pay off. You're still in a life phase where things can't be rushed, but you're starting to see progress. You may even be getting some extra encouragement as you watch the seeds of intention you have planted sprout and maybe even begin to bear fruit. Your patience is rewarded in people seeing you as dependable, thoughtful, and worth investing in.

### Love

When the Knight of Pentacles appears, you are most likely dealing with a partner who is trustworthy and loyal, someone you feel you can always count on. If it's a new relationship, however, you may need to take your time while you get to know each other. Your partner or love interest tends to be emotionally stable and predictable and will expect the same from you. In already committed partnerships, you are in a phase where you are ready to take things to the next stage of commitment. This can manifest in the form of a marriage proposal, deciding to start a family, or cementing your relationship by creating a home together. Whatever it is, it's done with intention and feels like a positive, productive movement forward.

## Career/Work

The Knight of Pentacles excels in readings that are focused around career and work because this is what he's good at. Money is accumulating slowly and steadily, and you are making progress; continue the good work because you're building toward greater success. You may find yourself needing to invest in your career goals in some way. Perhaps you are called to return to school or to take a class or seminar to deepen your knowledge of your profession, or you may link up with someone more knowledgeable who will become a mentor to you.

## Personal/Spiritual

The Knight of Pentacles represents a phase in life where you have found—or are very close to finding—the daily routine and regimen that works best for you. You are being guided to commit yourself to a plan that is realistic and practical while also paying attention to your personal growth and overall well-being and happiness. The appearance of the Knight of Pentacles reminds you to be mindful about your diet, consider the effect your environment has on you, and give thought to the people you are spending time with, because all of these play an important role in your growth. Set realistic goals for yourself and work toward them daily, realizing that small steps are significant and that the habits you form today create a lifestyle—make sure it's one that is positive and healthy for you.

## Reversed

When the Knight of Pentacles shows up reversed, your sense of security and structure is questionable. You might find that you are losing money or that you need to restructure your budget. You may also notice that the investments you made aren't presently paying off and your future plans are starting to look a little rocky. In relationship readings, someone you thought was a sure thing might be reconsidering the direction of the relationship or not willing to put the work in right now. Maybe it's not that they're not committed; it could be that they are distracted by outside influences like work responsibilities or stress in their personal life. Your patience is wearing thin, and you're wondering if all your effort is going to pay off.

QUEEN of PENTACLES.

## QUEEN OF PENTACLES

"I am the queen of practical thinking, abundance, and earthly riches."

The Queen of Pentacles represents a person who is both practical and sensual. She is concerned with material growth and stability for herself and for her family, and she enjoys time with family and close friends as much as she enjoys her time alone. Usually the Queen of Pentacles is someone who is a homemaker, owns a business, or has a career that involves tending to others. She is loyal and hardworking and enjoys living the life of luxury and comfort that she has worked so hard to create for herself.

## Love

When the Queen of Pentacles appears in a love reading, you are most likely dealing with someone who is down to earth, practical, nurturing, and very friendly. They give you solid advice and have a calm way about them. This person enjoys both being outside and being at home and is usually an excellent cook. It almost seems like anything the Queen of Pentacles touches will turn to gold because she not only has a nurturing energy about her but also has a connection to growth and fertility. When the Queen of Pentacles appears, you are being guided to take your time in selecting the right mate for yourself. There is no need to rush when it comes to finding someone worthy of committing yourself to, and the Queen of Pentacles understands that. You are most likely interested in creating a stable relationship with someone now or you are dealing with a person who wants that for themselves.

## Career/Work

In a work-related reading, the appearance of the Queen of Pentacles is an encouragement to make realistic, practical choices regarding your career; they will yield the greatest amount of growth. This card tells you to invest in yourself and the goals you have for your future. Create a plan or connect with a mentor who will advise you on the next best steps to take, and then dedicate yourself to achieving those goals. Don't expect success overnight; that will come from your dedication as you make progress and connections over time.

### Personal/Spiritual

In personal and spiritual matters, the Queen of Pentacles wants you to take yourself seriously and take care of yourself in the best way you know how. This card is all about balance. It is equal parts eating healthy, exercising, maintaining positive relationships with the people you care about the most, and doing things you truly love simply because you love them. You are working on manifesting your truest desires now, tending to them daily and giving them space for growth to occur effortlessly.

### Reversed

Reversed, the Queen of Pentacles starts to become materialistic, lazy, and dependent on others. She is no longer capable of making practical, realistic decisions—if she's even making decisions at all. It seems like growth has stopped for her and on what she has been working so hard to build; now she is in a space where she is wasting her resources and her money. She's second-guessing herself and might marry or partner with someone for the sake of what they can

financially give to her and not for love. She doesn't want to work hard anymore; she just wants to receive.

## KING OF PENTACLES

KING of PENTACLES.

"I am the king of practical advice; I provide stability and structure."

The King of Pentacles is a card of financial success, security, and stability. Because this suit is rooted in earth energy, he takes his time and approaches matters in ways that are practical and sensible. When he commits himself to something or someone, he is dedicated and, with gentle, loving devotion, will do whatever it takes to foster growth and success. For this reason, people want to work with him; he's knowledgeable and informed and will see tasks through to the end.

### Love

In matters of love, the King of Pentacles represents someone who is methodical, patient, loving, loyal, and kind. He makes an excellent partner and is someone you can

always count on. He would rather be partnered with someone who is equally as
committed as he is, and he's not going to
choose just anybody. When he does commit
himself to a partner, it's because he has
weighed all of their pros and cons and found
them worthy of giving them his full heart. He
is generous with his resources and will
always look out and provide for the people
he cares about while expecting nothing in
return. When the King of Pentacles shows up
in a romance spread, it may be because you
are looking for commitment and a partner to
build a future with. If you are in a relationship, you may be contemplating marriage,
creating a home, starting a family, or simply
be thinking very seriously about who you are
spending your time with.

## Career/Work

The appearance of the King of Pentacles
means that your hard work and dedication
are paying off in spades! Because you are
responsible, consistent, and committed to
your goals, you are going to see success
in your work life if you haven't already.
Oftentimes, the King of Pentacles shows up
to represent an important person who can
help move your career along; this person is
patient and kind and will help you whenever
you need it. The financial investments you're
now making will probably pay off. This card
is guiding you to take a realistic, practical

approach to decisions regarding your work
life; if you do, you will most likely see success.

## Personal/Spiritual

Good old common sense is what you need to
make the decisions in front of you concern-
ing your personal and/or spiritual life. You
are being reminded that success doesn't
happen overnight; it's usually achieved over
time. Have patience; make a plan to help
guide you toward your end goal. Ask for what
you know you are worthy of so that you can
create long-term security and stability. If you
are thinking about taking a risk, weigh the
pros and cons before you take a leap into the
unknown. Don't forget to take care of
yourself—in mind, body (including enjoying
the finer things in life), soul, and spirit.

## Reversed

The King of Pentacles reversed is stingy and
rigidly stubborn. His only focus is on accumulating money, and then he wants to show it
off to make others jealous of him. Oftentimes,
this card shows up for someone who is
spending more time at work than anywhere
else, and it's starting to eat away at their
relationships and their health. This person
ends up becoming self-indulgent and greedy.
He's not concerned with the well-being of
others, refuses to share, and will take
advantage of them if it serves his desires.

**SWORDS**

## PAGE OF SWORDS

*"We need to talk."*

The Page of Swords usually shows up to bring a message of change. It's questionable whether the news you receive will be something you want to hear. The Swords suit doesn't always bode well for your emotions because it doesn't stop to consider them. Its main focus is to tell you the truth. When the Page of Swords appears, the energy he brings is intellectual and logical. This energy can be forward, his bluntness unexpectedly aggressive. When this card appears, you know that you are going to receive communication from someone about a cold, hard truth.

## Love

The Page of Swords has a difficult time with love and relationships because he's not very good at expressing or even considering the feelings of others. He is driven more by logic, reason, and what intellectually makes sense rather than what feels good emotionally. This card can represent a date where the connection between you and the other person is more intellectual than romantic. If you expect it, you won't be disappointed by how the date unfolds. If you and your partner are having a serious conversation about what you each want for the relationship, the appearance of the Page of Swords means you are both speaking your truth to each other, no matter how hard it might be to hear.

## Career/Work

The appearance of the Page of Swords in the area of career and work signifies energy and an exchange that could require research or negotiation in a short time period. Maybe you are putting together a contract or other document for someone to sign that could initiate a new phase of development in your career. If you're waiting to hear back about a job or from clients, you're going to hear from them soon, but the news you receive could be either positive or negative—it's hard to tell with the Page of Swords.

### Personal/Spiritual

In personal readings, the Page of Swords encourages you to be inquisitive. This card is about teaching you to speak your truth even if it may rub people the wrong way or disappoint them. It is also about learning to accept the truth and not take anything personally. With the Page of Swords, the logical and rational are prioritized over the intuitive and emotional, and it's important for you to learn how to work with both in order to maintain balance in your life. Do your research before diving in, and don't be afraid to ask for additional details so that you have greater clarity about the things you are agreeing to.

### Reversed

When the Page of Swords is reversed, the news you were expecting is blocked and not coming through. Some tarot readers say that when the Page of Swords is reversed, he brings only bad news. That hasn't been my experience. I've seen the Page of Swords deliver negative news when upright, and when reversed, I've seen positive and negative information that's either delayed or never comes at all. When this card appears reversed, you want to be careful what you say because your words can be used against you. Others may interpret them as cruel or heartless (maybe they are!). That's the energy the Page of Swords brings when reversed.

## KNIGHT OF SWORDS

KNIGHT of SWORDS.

"I am the knight who brings unexpected messages."

The Knight of Swords bursts into a tarot reading like a gust of wind. It brings unexpected messages and information that may shock you or require that you act with speed. The energy of this card is forceful, focused, and unstoppable. If there is a message he needs to bring, he's going to do it quickly, so much so that it will leave your head spinning. Oftentimes, the Knight of Swords brings the energy of conflict because its energy is a little aggressive. When this card appears in a reading, prepare for highly animated conversations that need to be had with people who are very intelligent, informed, and have done their research.

### Love

The Knight of Swords is another card that is challenged when it comes to love relationships because it doesn't understand emotions that well, if at all. The Knight of Swords spends so much time in his head that he almost totally neglects his heart. If it doesn't logically make sense to him, he's not going to do it; in fact, he may not even have time for a relationship or intimacy right now. If this card represents a person you love, like, or are in a relationship with, you will find that the connection between you is very intellectually stimulating and that you have common goals you are working toward together. Communication is very important in regard to the question you're asking. If you ask your love interest or partner how they feel about you or what they want out of the relationship, be prepared for the answer because you're going to get the truth.

## Career/Work
When the Knight of Swords appears in a work-related reading, you need to be ready for action, challenges, and problem-solving. This is a time not only to do your research but also to make sure you have facts upon facts to support your findings. Others are going to challenge you, and you want to be prepared. There may be some adversity and friction in your work environment, but this card is suggesting that you see this as a challenge and not take it personally. Use your logic to make rational and reality-based decisions. Connect with others who are highly informed and knowledgeable and are not afraid to tell you the truth so that you can identify problems, fix them, and move forward without delay.

## Personal/Spiritual
In personal and spiritual readings when the Knight of Swords shows up, it is encouraging you to make decisions based upon facts and logic. You may have been relying heavily on your emotions and feelings, but those have a tendency to change or can sometimes lock you in a situation that you need to move away from. A logical approach will help you see the truth, even if it hurts the heart (yours or someone else's) to make a decision that is good for you at this time. The Knight of Swords knows exactly what you want, and you need to learn how to clearly articulate it to others so there will be no misunderstandings. This will nip any potential problems in the bud before they have a chance to develop into larger headaches.

## Reversed
Reversed, the Knight of Swords will hurt people with his honesty. This card is known for being decisive, but reversed, it comes across as harsh and almost cruel in its delivery. This knight will disagree for the sake of disagreeing, provoke a fight, and not back down or apologize. It could signify that someone is working against you, using their intellect to sabotage you, or working for evil purposes

instead of good. The Knight of Swords reversed could also refer to someone in your orbit who comes across as a know-it-all.

# QUEEN OF SWORDS

QUEEN of SWORDS.

"I am the queen of logic and rational thinking. I analyze and see all."

The Queen of Swords is a woman of independence who is emotionally detached yet is possessed of sound reason. She is highly intelligent and gifted in her ability to use rational thought to make decisions. Despite having gone through a lot, the Queen of Swords is able to disconnect from her feelings to make judgments that are logically sound. That is her gift. She is clear about her expectations and ambitions. Her work life and/or her projects are where she spends the majority of her time and attention.

## Love
When the Queen of Swords appears in a romantic reading, it may mean that you find yourself spending a lot of time alone or disconnected from others to focus on goals that don't involve intimacy and romantic relationships. This card shows up for someone who is preoccupied with a task or project that requires a lot of thought, energy, and effort, and so their love life tends to take a backseat for the time being. If you are in a relationship with someone, this card indicates that person is a bit emotionally distant and very cool in how they express their love and affection toward you. In fact, it can be hard to get a read on what they may be feeling for you, if anything. You may even have moments where you wonder if they even actually like you, but you might find it endearing and challenging rather than disappointing.

## Career/Work
The appearance of the Queen of Swords in a career-related question is a positive signifier, as this is the primary focus. The work she's doing now likely requires her full attention and time spent away from others, perhaps doing research in the fields of science, math, or medicine. When this card appears, you are in a place where you are using your rational thinking to succeed in your work environment. In fact, it seems as though letting your emotions/feelings get in the way of your work would be detrimental, so you are working to separate the two.

## Personal/Spiritual

The Queen of Swords in a personal reading is calling you to be a little less transparent with others about your feelings at this time. You are in a space where you are called to separate yourself from your emotions in order to make judgments that are for your highest and greatest good. Boundaries are very important now, as is articulating your expectations of others in a way that clears up any confusion. You are learning that your sole purpose in life is not to make others happy or to paint the truth in a pretty way because that's not how life always is. You are focused on your independence, doing what is right, and putting your head before your heart.

## Reversed

When the Queen of Swords is reversed, her heart has completely iced over. Not only does she not care about your feelings and her delivery of the truth, but she gets a sick pleasure out of hurting others with her words. She is negative and self-defeating, and she may use her power of intimidation to manipulate others to do things they don't want to do. She doesn't consider feelings, including her own, and it creates suffering for everyone. Reversed, this queen's need for independence turns into an unhealthy obsession with proving herself, and she ends up completely isolating herself from those who care about her. This woman is your worst enemy.

## KING OF SWORDS

KING of SWORDS.

"I am the king of logic and reason. I bring truth with law and order."

The King of Swords represents intelligence, logic, law and order, and intellectual decision-making. His mind is as sharp as his tongue. He says very little, but what he does say is clear and direct. He is a man of strength and doesn't back down for anyone. You will never find him making decisions based on what he feels—it will always come from what logically makes sense and is the right thing to do for everyone. His face doesn't really show emotion; he comes across as very cool and calculated. He is rigid in his ways and follows the rule book no matter what the circumstance is or who is involved.

## Love

The King of Swords struggles with intimacy and romance because that is not his forte. If he is in a romantic relationship, he doesn't spend much time thinking about it or engaging in it. The King of Swords and Queen of Swords are the cards that signify people most likely to spend their lives independent from a partner because they are very focused on their work and their convictions; they won't compromise in order to share their life with someone else. In fact, most people have a hard time connecting with them, and they kind of prefer that. If you are in a relationship with a King of Swords type of character, you'll need patience, acceptance, and understanding for this connection to survive. Don't expect this person to talk about their intimate feelings because it's just not going to happen. They're not comfortable with that level of intimacy, nor do they ever want to be—as far as they are concerned, it doesn't serve a purpose. If that works for you, then you can handle a relationship with a King of Swords.

## Career/Work

The King of Swords in a career reading signifies that you are dealing with a person or energy that requires an intellectual approach, rational decision-making, and professionalism. Your determination and motivation to work toward the goal must be focused; you can't allow distractions to pull you away from your desk and derail you.

Commit to your cause—totally devote yourself to your craft and the quality of your work. Use your head right now, not your heart.

## Personal/Spiritual

In personal and spiritual readings, the King of Swords brings up skeptical energy. You are questioning what is real, and you need proof that what you were taught to believe is true. The King of Swords insists on factual evidence, not blind faith. If it doesn't make sense to you, it simply won't work. Don't be afraid to do things alone.

## Reversed

When reversed, the King of Swords is using his power for evil. He is cruel, mean, and coldhearted. Think of any evil villain in a Disney movie, and that's the kind of energy the King of Swords reversed brings to the tarot table. His dominant nature is intimidating and terrifying. He will send a cold chill up your spine because he will do whatever is necessary to take or maintain power, and he will use that power to control others. His cold, calculated thinking means there is no hope of connecting with him or persuading him to consider the feelings of people who may still care about him. With the King of Swords reversed, people in his orbit are not there because they want to be but because he is manipulating them.

# WANDS

## PAGE OF WANDS

PAGE of WANDS.

"I am the sparkplug of the tarot, full of exciting ideas and ready for adventure!"

Just like all the pages, the Page of Wands is considered a messenger within the tarot deck. He's connected to fire, and so is passionate, filled with energy, and ambitious. He comes in with speed and excitement, and the news he brings tends to spark these types of feelings within you as well. This little guy is courageous, bold, and assertive despite being the youngest of the Wand Court Cards. He's not afraid to get his hands dirty or to start some new adventure that might be terrifying for others to take

on. His fearlessness inspires others to say yes to life!

### Love

In love readings, the Page of Wands brings excitement, passion, and fun . . . but not much else. I wouldn't expect too much from this card when it comes to long-term relationships because he's definitely not ready to settle down. Right now, he's exploring his options, and he finds you stunning, but you are just the prize of the moment. After that—all bets are off. This isn't necessarily bad if you are both on the same page with your expectations. The Page of Wands encourages you to explore your options, to pursue whatever sparks passion and light within you, and to be fearless in that pursuit.

### Career/Work

In career readings, the Page of Wands encourages you to take risks! To reap rewards, you have to put yourself out there, and the Page of Wands is supporting you in doing that. He's quick to learn, impatient and restless, and highly intelligent. Connect with others, get involved, and be courageous! Don't be afraid to switch things up and try something new—that's where you may actually find the most growth and potential in your work or business.

### Personal/Spiritual

In personal readings, the Page of Wands brings the same energy he does in a work-related or general reading. He's pushing you to get excited about life and to take action. Life is not meant to be monotonous, and at some point, you have to step outside your comfort zone and constructively seek what excites and challenges you. For people who always say no to everything, now is a good time to switch things up and say yes. Book that trip, get on that flight, pursue that dream. Now's the time!

### Reversed

The Page of Wands reversed brings reckless and childish energy. His normal spontaneous energy now seems impulsive, almost dangerous. He's taking risks for the sake of risk, and it will start to create problems that may be difficult or impossible to fix later. This person is not someone you can count on because he gets distracted, gives up, and fizzles out, abandoning projects midway through. In relationships, you might have thought it was love, but they'll be gone in the blink of an eye on to the next shiny object. The Page of Wands reversed brings disappointment and frustration more than anything else.

## KNIGHT OF WANDS

KNIGHT of WANDS.

*"I am passionate and ready to make bold changes!"*

The Knight of Wands is the older brother of the Page of Wands, a more mature version, representing excitement and new beginnings. This card usually brings a message or news from an accidental messenger about an important exciting event or about people who are entering your life now. The Knight of Wands is someone who is filled with energy, enthusiasm, and a sense of adventure. He's willing to take a risk but knows better than the Page of Wands which risks are worthwhile and which are simply reckless. This knight loves to have a good time, is very extroverted, and can often be found at a party, surrounded by others with similar energy who want to have a good time.

### Love

In matters of love, the Knight of Wands is here to have a good time. He is confident, charismatic, and a little cocky. He is either very popular or is entertaining a lot of people when he appears in your life. If you're single and this card shows up, you can expect a quick, passionate love affair, but it's debatable if it will last—though he will save your number and call when the mood strikes him. It's a "friends with benefits" type of situation. No matter what your plans are together, you will almost always end up getting physical because the Knight of Wands has a hard time keeping his hands to himself. In committed relationships, this is when that spark of passion and attraction is really strong between a couple, and they are enjoying this energy in their love life. You may be with a person who really challenges you, excites you, and makes you feel alive. Or maybe you are running away together spontaneously to enjoy each other's company. The Knight of Wands represents a partner who makes you laugh and puts a smile on your face.

## Career/Work

In career- and work-related readings, the Knight of Wands is passion ignited! He is fast moving, so he brings a message of change, adventure, and challenges you are excited to take on. In your work, you may be called upon to meet people from different cultures and backgrounds. You are thrilled by this because you learn so much by seeing different perspectives and being exposed to different walks of life. The risks you are taking now are exciting, and you can quickly see the reward. You are in a phase in your life where you are ready to get into the thick of things and prove yourself, and that's what others are calling for you to do.

## Personal/Spiritual

When the Knight of Wands appears in this area, you are encouraged to spice up your life in a way that is meaningful and significant for you. This card reminds you to have faith, believe in yourself, pursue what excites you feverishly, and never give up. The Knight of Wands is bold and confident, and that's the energy he wants you to bring to your own life now. Take a risk and receive the reward. Let your hair down and start to have fun. Don't take yourself or others too seriously because life is too short.

## Reversed

When the Knight of Wands shows up reversed, his enthusiastic need for challenge and change gets the best of him. His decision-making is impulsive, and everything he touches seems to break or backfire. Just like the reversed Page of Wands, the reversed Knight of Wands can't be counted on to get things done, and if he does, it's not going to be done well. He's the one most likely to take shortcuts or to present half-finished, sloppy work. This knight is quick to get in fights with others or to offend someone by what he does or says. Reversed in a love reading, he speeds in and speeds out and is only interested in sex. After that, he disappears and doesn't care if he breaks someone's heart.

## QUEEN OF WANDS

"I am the queen who brings charm, charisma, and faith in the future."

The Queen of Wands is outgoing, beautiful, exciting, and visually striking. She naturally draws people in because she's very animated and engaging. When she walks in a room, she turns heads because her energy is light; she is almost always smiling or chatty, and her confidence is very attractive. On her best day, the Queen of Wands is friendly and accepting of others. She is entertaining and quick to share a story or joke that can make people laugh and lighten the mood of the room. Normally she has a partner, but even in her relationship, she maintains her independence; she has her own identity and likes to keep it that way. If she is a mother, she is very fun loving and enjoys playing with her children and spending time outdoors. She also tends to be competitive in a way that is fun for all.

### Love
In matters of love, the Queen of Wands tends to be the life of the party. She's open-minded, loves to have a good time, is not one to stay still, and enjoys a partner who can keep up with her—even challenge her! She's quick to feel boredom and likes to be on the go doing the things she loves (she has so many different interests), and she wants to share these with the person she cares about. Even though she turns heads because of her magnetic personality, when she finds the right person, she's very loyal to them.

### Career/Work
In career- and work-related readings, the Queen of Wands shines! She is most likely in charge of others or running the entire organization. She is similar to the Queen of Pentacles in that way, but they differ in that the Queen of Wands is more likely to be out and about, engaging and making public appearances, while the Queen of Pentacles is more restrained and has a tendency to stay behind her desk. When this card appears, it's calling on you to believe in yourself, to learn how to engage with others, to independently pursue the things that excite you, and to

share them with others so they can see your potential. If you have a business plan or idea, take the steps needed to get the ball rolling, believe that you can do it, and then make the dream a reality. The Queen of Wands knows her potential is limitless, and abundant opportunities tend to show up because she attracts them and is confident enough to say yes to them.

## Personal/Spiritual

In personal readings, the Queen of Wands asks you to be confident and share your light with others as well as your ideas. Don't hold your enthusiasm back. You're at a point in your life where you are getting a chance to infuse new meaning and adventure into your everyday activities. You may find yourself signing up for a class to learn something new or trying something you've never done before, and then meeting new friends and expanding your social circle in the process. If there is a trip you want to take or a goal you would love to achieve, it's never too late to get started. You never know where your passions can take you—the Queen of Wands understands this and is excited by your potential!

## Reversed

Reversed, the Queen of Wands is obnoxious, to say the least. She needs constant attention and will do whatever it takes to have all eyes on her, no matter the cost. She tends to be bossy and is a notorious "mean girl." She talks about people behind their backs and loves to gossip and find out the personal details of someone's life only to share them with their enemy at some point. She uses her charismatic personality to entrap people just to say that she can do it. She's not afraid to break up friendships or marriages for the sake of her own ego. She can react in ways that can be violent or downright scary. There's no way she is actually interested in anything you're saying unless it serves her own purpose or evil intentions. A reversed Queen of Wands thrives off making others feel less than her, and she wants people to glorify and lift her up even if she doesn't deserve it.

## KING OF WANDS

KING of WANDS.

"I am the king who brings passion, adventure, and positivity."

Just like his counterpart, the King of Wands tends to be the life of the party.

He's loud in a fun way, and he's always ready to have a good time. The King of Wands has a strong presence about him as well, and others know when he enters a room because he most likely just announced it. He's funny, confident, ambitious, and very knowledgeable and accepting of everyone. He's not quick to judge others; he will seek to understand and accept you as you are. He has so many stories about his life adventures, and I can guarantee you that he has a shelf full of medals and trophies. As much as he loves to talk about himself, he is equally excited to connect with others and is very generous. He's known for his optimism and for his ability to breathe life into people, especially when they need it most. The King of Wands is the guy who is always up for adventure and says yes to any challenge that comes his way simply because he loves it.

## Love

In love relationships, the King of Wands is passionate, exciting, loyal, and a strong provider. He's someone you know you will have a good time with; with him by your side, you know you will enjoy what life has to offer. He doesn't like monotony, so he's going to want to change things up. Just know that you will be kept on your toes if you enter into a relationship with the King of Wands.

Optimism and a positive attitude are very important to him—he cannot stand a person who says no or doesn't want to even leave the house. The King of Wands is ready to go out and conquer and feels as though life is meant to be experienced. He's someone you can trust and count on, and you know that if you call him, he will always make you laugh.

## Career/Work

In career-related readings, the King of Wands is the leader, naturally. He usually does work that involves travel or sales. He knows everyone, has a wide network of connections, and can help you with anything you need. Somehow, he manages to maintain human bonds for years, and everyone considers him a close friend. This card wants you to be assertive and to take a leadership role in your career. The King of Wands knows that you can do it and that the time has come. Market yourself in a way that highlights your strengths, because now is not a time to be to humble. Let others see your skills and strengths!

## Personal/Spiritual

The King of Wands assures you that now is the time for you to start that new venture, explore your world, or commit yourself to something you love and are passionate about. The King of Wands knows exactly what he wants so he will hold on to it and cherish it when he sees it. Believe in yourself and work daily to encourage yourself through the power of positive thinking and words of affirmations. Spend time outdoors doing the things you love simply for the enjoyment of doing them, not for the achievement of any particular purpose or goal.

## Reversed

When the King of Wands is reversed, his energy is blocked or off balance. This is when his ego spirals out of control—he is overconfident, destructive, and overly dominant. He doesn't care about how others feel because he's only concerned with what makes him feel good. Reversed, he morphs into someone who is bossy, just like the Queen of Wands reversed becomes a bit of a bully. He surrounds himself with people who are weak or followers because he loves when people feed his ego.

# 6

# SOME SPREADS TO GET YOU STARTED

**A**S IF LEARNING AND REMEMBERING THE meaning of the cards weren't enough, now I'm asking you to dive into the tarot spreads, which can be complex all by itself! The reality is that without a tarot spread, you'll have a whole lot of confusion and chaos because the cards will be thrown down without any rhyme or reason. That's the beauty and purpose of using a tarot spread; it creates structure for the reading so that it flows effortlessly. When you familiarize yourself with the spreads, you'll be able to understand what the placement of each card means, and you'll give the best reading of your life (ideally) again and again!

A tarot spread is kind of like a map, and each spot (card) on that map shows you what you will discover there. For example, a lot of spreads have what is called an outcome position that shows what most likely will happen if things continue as they are and don't change—and you then get to decide if that is the destination you want to arrive at or not.

Don't be intimidated by reading spreads—it's just another tool for you to use in your tarot journey. Let's dive into some of my favorite spreads and the ones I use most often.

# ONE-CARD DRAW

Don't underestimate the One-Card Draw because it looks simple. This spread is actually quite powerful to work with! In fact, I find myself asking a question and shuffling with this spread a lot, and it always serves me well. Use this spread when you need a clear, concise answer to a question. You can also use it for questions regarding timing, like if you want to know when something will happen (if it will happen at all).

## What the Positions Mean

There is only one position within this spread, and the potential for what this spread represents is endless! For example, if you are asking how someone feels about you, it represents their feelings. If you ask when you'll receive a text message or phone call, it represents the time it takes for that message to come in.

## Tips for Interpreting This Spread

Before you shuffle, know exactly what it is that you're asking to help understand the card when it is pulled. I recommend working with the One-Card Draw daily—or as often as you can—by asking what to expect from the day or what messages you need to pay attention to.

# THREE-CARD SPREAD: PAST, PRESENT, FUTURE

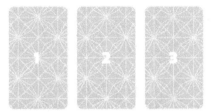

Use the Three-Card Spread for focusing on what has happened and what is going to happen. Don't use this spread if you are trying to ask the cards for advice or insight into your situation. For example, if I'm going on a trip that I'm feeling nervous about, I'll use this spread and pull cards so I can plan.

## What the Positions Mean

**POSITION 1:** The past. This is where you have come from and what has occurred. Usually this is something you can confirm because it has just happened.

**POSITION 2:** The present. This is the energy around you now and what is currently happening. If a Court Card appears, this is showing you who is influencing your question and what type of energy they bring.

**POSITION 3:** The future. This shows what you can expect to happen next. Make sure to determine timing for this placement within

the spread, so you'll know when something is most likely to occur. For example, when you are shuffling the cards, clearly say, "I want to know what is going to manifest in the next three to four months." If you forget to do this, shuffle the deck and pull a clarifying card with the intention of finding out the timing

## Tips for Interpreting This Spread

Remember that the Three-Card Spread is designed to reveal what has happened, what is happening, and what will happen . . . nothing more than that. Stay open-minded because anything can happen; the cards will do their best to communicate as fluently as they can to you. Don't try to guess what they are saying. Sometimes it's best to see these cards, make a note of them, and then confirm afterward (especially for the card that represents the future!) what the cards were trying to say.

# CELTIC CROSS

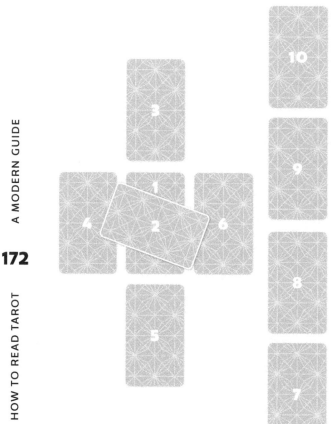

The Celtic Cross is one of the most commonly used spreads, and for good reason: It does an amazing job of delving deeply into whatever you are asking about! Use this spread when you really want to know and understand what is happening around one specific question or issue. For example, if you are struggling to find out why there is a feeling of icy coolness between you and your best friend, you can use this spread to find out what has happened and what is going on now. This spread is a gem because it covers almost everything you could possibly need to know to understand an issue and what you can do to change it for the better. It's a very empowering spread!

## What the Positions Mean

**POSITION 1:** This card sums up your reading overall. So, in a nutshell, this card's position shows you the question in its entirety—not to be confused with the outcome or the querent (aka the person who's asking the question).

**POSITION 2:** The things or people that are supporting you or opposing you. This means what is helping your outcome to manifest in the way you desire and what is working against it. With this position, keep an open mind because something that seems like it's a positive could actually be a problem that you're not fully aware of, so you want to look at the rest of the cards within the reading before settling on its true meaning.

**POSITION 3:** The foundation of the question. In other words, why it is you asked the question in the first place. In most readings, this gives a general idea of where the person is at the time they are asking the question and what their ulterior motives are.

**POSITION 4:** The past and what has just recently occurred at the time the question is asked. This is usually something you can confirm because it's already happened; it's also an awesome moment for the reader and the querent to bond because it builds trust when the reader nails exactly what just happened for the querent!

**POSITION 5:** The energy around you in the form of potential. Oftentimes, this shows what the querent is hoping for. Because they're hoping for it, there's a chance it will manifest, depending on what is working for or against them.

**POSITION 6:** Here we see what is most likely to happen next—especially the things we can't control. Sometimes this is a curveball, and other times it's expected. If you know what is coming, you can at least begin to prepare for it.

**POSITION 7:** The person asking the question and the energy they bring to the reading.

**POSITION 8:** Outside aspects and influences: usually another person if the question is about someone else.

**POSITION 9:** This space is for your guides to give you advice about what Spirit thinks is the best way to attain your desired outcome. I look at this as an open door in the reading for our guides to speak to us and deliver messages we might have missed otherwise.

**POSITION 10:** This is the outcome position within the spread. When all things are considered, this is the most likely outcome if everything continues as is. Keep in mind that you can change this if you don't like what you see here—the power is in your hands!

## Tips for Interpreting This Spread

When working with the Celtic Cross, first examine each position within the spread individually, and then take a step back and look at the bigger picture. This will help you deeply understand what the tarot is showing you and put the pieces together to understand the greater picture. I've noticed that new readers sometimes walk away from the Celtic Cross having only a general understanding but still need to go further. This is simply because they are looking at each detail individually and neglect the reading's vibe as a whole.

## 21-CARD SPREAD

| 7 | 6 | 5 | 4 | 3 | 2 | 1 |

| 14 | 13 | 12 | 11 | 10 | 9 | 8 |

| 21 | 20 | 19 | 18 | 17 | 16 | 15 |

Use the 21-Card Spread when you want to cover all aspects of your life right now. This spread is good for when you want to see what's developing around you and you might not have a specific question in mind. The levels of layering that occur within this tarot spread will give you specifics on what you can expect in each section. If you do have a specific question, you can ask that, and it will dive into the energy surrounding whatever it is you're inquiring about. This spread will reveal the ways in which you can manifest what you want or change the outcome of your current situation to best match your desires or goals.

## What the Positions Mean

**POSITIONS 1, 8, AND 15:** These show your current status as far as where your head is, your energy, and your expectations.

**POSITIONS 2, 9, AND 16:** These represent the environment around you. This usually symbolizes the things you can't control but have an influence over. There are other people involved, and this is the energy they bring.

**POSITIONS 3, 10, AND 17:** These reveal your expectations and hopes—what you would like to see manifest. If you are experiencing negative thinking, you can also see that here. This is important because it gives greater understanding into your mind-set and how your own influence is blocking or building energy around the question.

**POSITIONS 4, 11, AND 18:** These show what has already occurred and what is on your mind.

**POSITIONS 5, 12, AND 19:** These will reveal unexpected developments or things hidden around the question. You need to take these into consideration to have a better understanding of the energy around them.

**POSITIONS 6, 13, AND 20:** These will reveal what is going to occur in the near future.

**POSITIONS 7, 14, AND 21:** These will show you the outcome when all things are considered. This is where you will most likely end up if things continue as they are.

## Tips for Interpreting This Spread

The 21-Card Spread is another spread where you want to take time to examine the details and the specifics of each section first, and then take a step back and look at the greater picture. This will help you develop a deeper understanding of what is truly unfolding in your life.

# WHEEL OF FORTUNE

After the Celtic Cross, the Wheel of Fortune is one of my favorite spreads to work with. It breaks down every aspect of each category of life and is inspired by astrology charts. Just like in the astrology or natal chart, each section represents a major aspect of one area of our lives. Traditionally, I work with the spread once a month to predict what I can expect to unfold over the next 30 days so

that I can plan accordingly. Then I do a separate reading once a year to predict the same thing for the next 365 days.

## What the Positions Mean

The Wheel of Fortune spread is inspired by astrology, so each card mirrors each house found within an astrology chart. Here is what they represent:

**POSITION 1:** Mirrors the house of self and, within the spread, shows the energy you bring to your environment and how you are coming across to the world.

**POSITION 2:** What is most valuable and important to you; can also show your financial future.

**POSITION 3:** Communication, the mind, and your connection to your brothers and sisters or your neighborhood. If you're traveling, you may also see hints of that here.

**POSITION 4:** Your home environment and your emotional needs.

**POSITION 5:** Your ability to create, date, and have fun. Children can be found here as well.

**POSITION 6:** Your daily routine, the quality of your health, and aspects of your work environment that involve daily tasks and annoyances.

**POSITION 7:** The potential to pair up in business partnerships or romantic relationships; reveals developments in your love life—for good or for bad.

**POSITION 8:** Major areas of personal transformation.

**POSITION 9:** What you will be learning and exploring, but also what your spiritual growth will look like.

**POSITION 10:** Your career, reputation, and work life. If there are major changes within your work environment, look to the cards in positions 6 and 10 to reveal what those changes might look like.

**POSITION 11:** Major hopes and wishes and if any of them will be fulfilled at this time; also represents friendships and social networking, so if you see any Court Cards show up, this can reveal special people in your life who will make a lasting impact.

**POSITION 12:** Your limitations and the things that hold you back. If you need rest and retreat, it will show what that will look like.

## Tips for Interpreting This Spread

When working with the Wheel of Fortune, I highly recommend pulling clarifying and advice cards for each section to help you work with the good and the bad of each category. Your tarot cards (and spirit guides) are always excited to help guide you, but they can only do that if you're asking for it. This spread is awesome for revealing each category of your life in detail, but it lacks a space to give advice to help things unfold. However, if you pull clarifying cards with the intent of gaining additional advice, you can take this spread's magick and potential to the next level!

# FIVE-CARD SPREAD

The Five-Card Spread is an extension of the Three-Card Spread, only it provides a little extra support and advice to help you move your goals along. You'll still see the past, the present, and the outcome, but you'll also receive advice about things that may be working against you, so you can prepare for it now. Use this spread when you want to predict how events are going to unfold but also need guidance about helping things move along in the ways you want.

## What the Positions Mean

**POSITION 1:** This card shows what you are recently exiting out of, so it represents the past. It is what has just happened and what is passing.

**POSITION 2:** This is the current situation around you or your question now.

**POSITION 3:** This is the future and what will unfold next.

**POSITION 4:** This card is a chance for your spirit guides to give you advice on what they think is best for you and what action you should take.

**POSITION 5:** This shows the most likely outcome if everything continues as is. As with any outcome card, you have the power to change it if you don't like the direction you're walking in.

## Tips for Interpreting This Spread

A little tip I can give you when working with the Five-Card Spread is to open the door to communication with your spirit guides by calling them in and giving them permission to advise you about what they see is best for you. You may have a specific outcome you want to manifest, and Spirit may hold a key that will help steer you in the direction of your highest and greatest good. Stay open to the guidance your guides give you, even if it may not make sense initially. Capture your reading in your tarot journal so that you can revisit it later and see clearly what they were suggesting at the time.

# HORSESHOE SPREAD

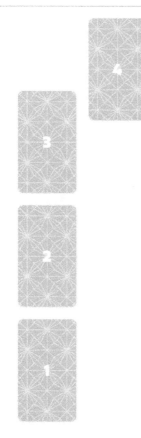

The Horseshoe is another spread that is super helpful for looking into the energy around your question; it is also excellent for those who need a little extra help with decision-making. Use this for asking specific questions when you can already see or feel obstacles around you. Just like the horseshoe, this spread is designed to change your luck for the better by giving you tools to better understand what you are up against.

## What the Positions Mean

**POSITION 1:** Past influences and circumstances.

**POSITION 2:** Your current influences and the energy around you or your question now.

**POSITION 3:** What the near future holds; what you can expect to develop or happen next.

**POSITION 4:** Advice from Spirit or the tarot—things they want you to know for your own good.

**POSITION 5:** Those around you and the energy they bring (this may or may not be important to you).

**POSITION 6:** Any opposition or obstacles that are working against you now.

**POSITION 7:** The most likely outcome if things continue as they are.

## Tips for Interpreting This Spread

The Horseshoe Spread is wonderful because it focuses on the problems as well as the potentials. Use this to your advantage by paying special attention to the advice the cards are giving you. If you do, you will feel super prepared for anything the universe tries to throw at you!

# DECISION-MAKING SPREAD

The Decision-Making Spread is used for the times in your life where you find yourself at a crossroads and you need help making a decision. It happens to the best of us— your intuition feels clouded, you feel overwhelmed, or maybe you just really need a little extra confirmation about what you've already decided. This spread will help you weigh your pros and cons while stimulating your intuition so that you feel guided in your knowledge of what you should do next.

## What the Positions Mean

**POSITION 1:** You and the energy you are currently bringing to the question asked at this moment.

**POSITIONS 2 AND 3:** The advantages if you decide to do A.

**POSITIONS 4 AND 5:** The challenges or disadvantages if you decide to do A.

**POSITIONS 6 AND 7:** The advantages if you decide to do B.

**POSITIONS 8 AND 9:** The challenges or disadvantages if you decide to do B.

**POSITION 10:** The outcome and what you will most likely do, knowing all you know now.

## Tips for Interpreting This Spread

When working with the Decision-Making Spread, think about your options and ask for clarity and confirmation into what your heart and intuition know about what is truly for your highest and greatest good. This spread is designed to help you connect with your own intuition and internal guidance so it's not going to give you advice as far as what you should do—that is something you get to decide for yourself once you understand the pros and cons of the situation.

# LOVE AND ROMANCE SPREAD

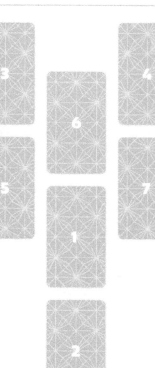

Use the Love and Romance Spread for new or established relationships to help two people connect deeper in their partnership, understand what they can expect for their future, and learn what they can do to work through any issues or blockages present or building up now.

## What the Positions Mean

**POSITION 1:** The energy of the relationship now as a whole. If it can summed up in one card, this would be it!

**POSITION 2:** The foundation of the relationship, whether it is stable, rocky, growing, or stagnant.

**POSITION 3:** The current health or potential of the relationship.

**POSITION 4:** Where the relationship is headed now.

**POSITION 5:** The recent past history of this relationship.

**POSITION 6:** The goals, hopes, and wishes for the relationship.

**POSITION 7:** The future of the relationship.

**POSITION 8:** Advice Spirit wants to impart to you to help this relationship unfold in a way that is for its highest and greatest good.

## Tips for Interpreting This Spread
A fun tip when using the Love and Romance Spread and love readings in general is to keep a photo nearby of the person you are inquiring about (whoever is in the relationship—new or old). This will help you connect instantly with their energy and will cancel out the tarot's ability to pick up on any love interest in the area when you are only inquiring about one person in particular. If you don't have any one specific person you are asking about, you don't need a photo—the tarot will scan the environment for budding love energy that could be on the horizon for you.

**185**

# MONEY- AND GOAL-BUILDING SPREAD

We could all benefit from a little more abundance to line our pockets or an extra boost of energy to manifest a goal. The Money- and Goal-Building Spread is designed to help with that. Not only will you see your earning potential, but you will also gain clarity into how you can best increase your reward or progress. This spread isn't just about accruing money but about exploring your relationship with it. If you understand your limits and restrictions, you can learn to work with them or around them . . . or maybe learn to remove them all together! This spread shows you your potential and what you need to do to progress forward.

## What the Positions Mean

**POSITION 1:** You and what your ability to attract, receive, keep, and build money looks like. If you are focused on a goal, this card shows the amount of energy you can currently give toward that goal.

**POSITION 2:** Your earning and growth potential.

**POSITION 3:** Your recent past regarding money and goals. For abundance readings, it shows your mind-set toward money.

**POSITION 4:** Blockages that are stopping your growth now.

**POSITION 5:** What you need to do or learn to move toward growth.

## Tips for Interpreting This Spread

When shuffling for the Money- and Goal-Building Spread, it really helps to think about your end goal and not the obstacles that will stand in your way. Where do you ideally see yourself financially? Ask your guides to show you how you can move in that direction. Just like with the law of attraction, if you focus on lack for this reading, you will receive an answer that supports that.

# TAROT CARD
# QUICK REFERENCE CHARTS

## Major Arcana Card Meanings

| CARD | UPRIGHT KEYWORDS | REVERSED KEYWORDS |
|---|---|---|
| 0. The Fool | innocence, naivete, fresh starts, new beginnings | recklessness, irresponsibility, foolishness, fear-bound |
| I. The Magician | initiation, self-mastery, power, intention, focus, magick | manipulation, powerlessness, conniving, con artist |
| II. The High Priestess | intuition, secret knowledge, unconscious mind | ignoring intuition, secret enemies |
| III. The Empress | growth, effortless attraction, beauty, feminine energy | stagnation, clinginess, drained energy, low self-worth |
| IV. The Emperor | authority, power, control, masculine energy, structure | abuse of power, forcing your will on others, immaturity |
| V. The Hierophant | tradition, following the rules, following the advice of elders or the wise ones | rejecting tradition, the abnormal, not fitting in, intolerance |
| VI. The Lovers | choice, union, love, partnership | indecision, a split or breakup, fear of commitment |
| VII. The Chariot | movement, travel, intention matched with purpose, determination | imbalance, stagnation, out of control, scattered energy, chaos |
| VIII. Strength | confidence, strength, discipline, patience | overly controlling, low self-esteem, weakness |
| IX. The Hermit | self-reflection, alone time, meditation, pulling away from the rest of the world | isolation, loneliness, disconnection from others or the inner self, escapism |
| X. Wheel of Fortune | fate, divine timing, good luck, nothing lasts forever—good or bad | bad luck, a turn for the worse, no movement forward |

| CARD | UPRIGHT KEYWORDS | REVERSED KEYWORDS |
| --- | --- | --- |
| XI. Justice | cross-examination, law and order, deliberation, finding fairness | unfairly judged, "getting away with murder," unjust outcomes, things not being fair |
| XII. The Hanged Man | suspension, letting go of control, trust, enlightenment, sacrifice | martyrdom, refusing to surrender, struggle, end of indecision |
| XIII. Death | total transformation, cleansing, release, powerful change | resisting change, holding on to the past, rot |
| XIV. Temperance | merging of opposites, alchemy, balance, calmness, harmony, polar opposites | excess, imbalance, overindulgence, clashing polarities, extreme conditions or mind-sets |
| XV. The Devil | temptation, attraction, commitments, binding agreements, attachment | unhealthy attachments, obsession, temptation that leads to disaster, breaking free |
| XVI. The Tower | surprise, disruption, dismantling the status quo, shock, a crisis, sudden developments | the surprise is lessened or not as extreme, rebuilding after drastic change, picking up the pieces of your life |
| XVII. The Star | healing, hope, inspiration, guidance, astrology, "light at the end of the tunnel," finding peace, trust | looking for a sign, feeling hopeless or lost, disillusionment |
| XVIII. The Moon | shadow self, deception, fantasy, illusion, emotional sensitivities, fear, confusion | learning the truth, seeing things for what they are, emotional extremes, destructive mood swings, drug use, deception |
| XIX. The Sun | joy, happiness, success, reward, celebration, positive energy, children, play, good health | delayed or overwhelmed by success, egocentric, loss of energy, needing recovery |
| XX. Judgement | resurrection, a rite of passage, awakening, hearing the final verdict | running from major changes, separation, forcing an outcome |
| XXI. The World | completion, the end of a journey, graduation, international connections, global travel | failure, inability to move forward, needing to backtrack, delays, obstacles |

# Minor Arcana Card Meanings: Cups

| CARD | UPRIGHT KEYWORDS | REVERSED KEYWORDS |
|---|---|---|
| Ace of Cups | birth, new love, romance, affection, intimacy, new relationship | emotional sensitivity, sadness, feelings blocked or left unexpressed, feeling empty |
| Two of Cups | union, partnership, mutual attraction, love, relationships, commitment | breakups, unrequited love, separation, imbalance in relationships |
| Three of Cups | celebration, people coming together, enjoying the moment, parties | love triangles, overindulgence |
| Four of Cups | boredom, stagnation, disinterest | emotional numbness, returning to passions, finding motivation again |
| Five of Cups | sadness, depression, pessimism, loss | settling for less, extended grief, regret |
| Six of Cups | memories, nostalgia, people from the past | skeletons in your closet, memories that haunt you, clinging to the past |
| Seven of Cups | having multiple options, brainstorming, lost in your thoughts | having too many options, the inability to choose or focus |
| Eight of Cups | saying goodbye, lack of fulfillment, sadness | returning for a second chance, refusing to move on, lingering in a hurtful situation |
| Nine of Cups | "your wish come true," contentment, satisfaction | overindulgence, a gift that comes at a price, feeling smug |
| Ten of Cups | family support, love, happily ever after | feeling unsupported, delayed emotional fulfillment, the heart feels incomplete |

# Minor Arcana Card Meanings: Pentacles

| CARD | UPRIGHT KEYWORDS | REVERSED KEYWORDS |
|------|------------------|-------------------|
| Ace of Pentacles | the first investment, sowing your seeds, commitment, a financial or job offer, reward | financial loss, breakdown of commitments, poor planning, bad investments, running out of resources |
| Two of Pentacles | juggling, multitasking, balancing | running out of resources, being overwhelmed, dropping the ball |
| Three of Pentacles | job well done, recognition, working with others | shortcuts, lack of ambition, lack of support or resources |
| Four of Pentacles | saving up, financial security, not budging or moving from the status quo, stubbornness | being defensive, miserly, refusing to share, set in your ways |
| Five of Pentacles | poverty, helplessness, falling on bad times | unable to find a job or help, financial strain worsens, surviving off the bare minimum |
| Six of Pentacles | sharing, helping others, giving and taking | debt collectors, selfish people, help that comes at a price |
| Seven of Pentacles | patience, evaluating your commitments, assessing the quality of your work | giving up on your work, not seeing the payoff, wasted energy |
| Eight of Pentacles | paying attention to detail, working on a project or goal with greater focus | taking shortcuts, looking for the easy way out, refusing to work hard, overworking yourself |
| Nine of Pentacles | financial security, independence, self-sufficiency | a loss in finances, being dependent on others, feeling isolated |
| Ten of Pentacles | financial abundance, wealth, security, stability | success or wealth that comes crashing down, loss of security, a lost inheritance |

# Minor Arcana Card Meanings: Swords

| CARD | UPRIGHT KEYWORDS | REVERSED KEYWORDS |
|---|---|---|
| Ace of Swords | power of the mind and word, assertiveness, focus, mental determination, logic, cutting things out of your life | words that destroy, negative thinking, cruelty or abuse |
| Two of Swords | stalemate, a pause, emotional suppression | release, a decision that is made, facing your feelings |
| Three of Swords | heartache, suffering, disappointment | pain that lingers on, recovery, healing |
| Four of Swords | rest, healing, renewal, self-care | avoiding taking a break, no time off, worn out, beat down |
| Five of Swords | ego, negative energy and people, betrayal, aggressive people | backstabbing, slander, violence, being humiliated |
| Six of Swords | moving forward, leaving the worst behind you, actual travel (especially on a boat) | plans to leave aborted, feeling stuck, having no way out |
| Seven of Swords | lying, stealing, or cheating; moving from place to place; hiding away | apologies, what was lost is now returned, getting ripped off |
| Eight of Swords | self-imposed restrictions, fear, pessimism | paralyzing fear, regaining control of your life, practicing mindfulness |
| Nine of Swords | panic attacks, insomnia, illness, fear, anxiety attacks | obsessive thinking, poor mental health, hallucinating |
| Ten of Swords | the end, rock bottom, the worst is over | pain that lingers on or is exaggerated, suffering that seems to never end, finding the light at the end of the tunnel |

# Minor Arcana Card Meanings: Wands

| CARD | UPRIGHT KEYWORDS | REVERSED KEYWORDS |
| --- | --- | --- |
| Ace of Wands | excitement, a new adventure or enterprise, passion, initiative | losing energy, the spark dies out, loss of interest, failure, powerlessness, lack of inspiration, no good ideas |
| Two of Wands | exploring your options, waiting, looking toward the future | losing hope, frustrating delays, zero progress |
| Three of Wands | waiting for something/someone to arrive, business taking off, international connections | plans that fall apart, unreliability, delays |
| Four of Wands | celebration, stability, setting down roots | a broken home, canceled plans or party, struggle to find peace |
| Five of Wands | competition, welcome challenges, needing to prove yourself | unwelcome competition, losing to others, tired of needing to prove yourself |
| Six of Wands | success, fame, being celebrated | attention that goes to your head, failure, feeling unappreciated |
| Seven of Wands | standing your ground, sticking up for yourself, not giving up | being taken advantage of, giving up, weakness, losing to others |
| Eight of Wands | speed, messages coming in quickly, travel | delays with travel and movement, miscommunication, having to reroute |
| Nine of Wands | being defensive, self-protection, believing in yourself | being defenseless, feeling weak, becoming a victim |
| Ten of Wands | burden, responsibility, a heavy workload | unable to carry on, losing your ambition, unbearable stress |

# Court Card Meanings

| CARD | UPRIGHT KEYWORDS | REVERSED KEYWORDS |
| --- | --- | --- |
| Page of Cups | a crush or first date, sharing feelings, creative inspiration | moodiness, depression, the brokenhearted |
| Knight of Cups | true love, a proposal, creative expression, falling in love | deception, someone who lies, escapism, drug abuse, poor mental health |
| Queen of Cups | nurturing, tending to others and yourself, following your heart | self-absorption, needing validation, clingy, smothering |
| King of Cups | being kind and compassionate, trustworthy, emotional stability | sleazy people, addiction, escapism, emotional immaturity |
| Page of Pentacles | learning, hearing news of a job offer, patience | wasted resources, laziness, stubbornness |
| Knight of Pentacles | dependable, practical, focus on building finances or securing commitments | lack of planning, greed, wasted effort |
| Queen of Pentacles | growth in business, enjoying the fruits of your labor, reliable people | laziness, overindulgence, shallowness, wasting resources |
| King of Pentacles | concerned with business and maintaining security, wealth, patience, generosity | being cheap, poor money management, scamming people |
| Page of Swords | curiosity, constructive criticism, news that can upset you | gossip, receiving bad news, hurtful words |
| Knight of Swords | mental activity and challenges, witty conversations, intellectual people | chaos, confusion, injustice, poor judgment |
| Queen of Swords | headstrong, using logic and reasoning, standing alone | cold, calculated, vindictive people |
| King of Swords | rational advice, using your head instead of your heart, focus on justice | violent people, being prejudiced, hungry for power no matter the cost |

| CARD | UPRIGHT KEYWORDS | REVERSED KEYWORDS |
|---|---|---|
| Page of Wands | daring, optimism, courage, staying active | impulsive behavior, impatience, attention seeking |
| Knight of Wands | changes happening quickly, excitement, not ready to settle down | impatience, recklessness, risky behavior |
| Queen of Wands | independent people, living your life to the fullest, having confidence | bossy, arrogant, needing to be the center of attention all the time |
| King of Wands | adventure, inspirational speaker, motivation | egocentrism, rage, aggression |

# INDEX

# ABOUT THE AUTHOR

**JESSICA WIGGAN** is a professional astrologer, intuitive, and reader based in New Orleans. She has more than 20 years' experience in reading and teaching tarot as well as 11 years of experience in the study of astrology. She is best known for her insightful and powerful readings while delivering channeled messages in an honest and uplifting way, as well as creating magick oil blends in the BehatiLife Apothecary during every new and full moon for her clients. Her mission is to be in service to others and the Divine and to spread love, healing, and light to all. You can find her on Instagram, YouTube, at her home base shop, BehatiLife.com, and on Facebook @BehatiLife.